P9-DCU-165

HOW TO HAVE OUTRAGEOUS FINANCIAL ABUNDANCE IN NO TIME

BIBLICAL PRINCIPLES FOR IMMEDIATE AND OVERWHELMING FINANCIAL SUCCESS

FRANCIS JONAH

TABLE OF CONTENTS

IMPORTANT

My name is Francis Jonah. I believe all things are possible. It is because of this belief that I have achieved so much in life. This belief extends to all. I believe every human being is equipped to succeed in every circumstance, regardless of the circumstance.

I know the only gap that exists between you and what you need to achieve or overcome is knowledge.

People are destroyed for lack of knowledge.

It is for this reason that I write short practical books that are so simple, people begin to experience immediate results as evidenced by the many testimonies I receive on daily basis for my various books.

This book is no exception. You will obtain results because of it. This book is only longer because your finances are sure to boom with such magnitude as you have never seen before.

Send me an email for a **FREE** copy of my book

"All Things Are Possible"

My email is drfrancisjonah@gmail.com

INTRODUCTION

When does a man experience financial prosperity? In my own experience, immediately.

When I made in a week what many make in a month, I realized I had finally cracked the financial abundance code. I had found the keys to financial abundance. I went on to multiply my annual income by five that year.

The core of the book starts from chapter five. The preceding chapters are a necessary foundation. In the ending chapters you will learn a costly mistake to avoid.

It was surprising what brought about that change. It was simple revelations from the word of God. Revelations you will receive in this book

Have you been poor before? I have. To live in a place where poverty was normal shapes your thinking differently. To live with parents who thought poverty was normal is one of the handicaps any person can face in life.

Your thinking and beliefs all align to bring poverty your way just because of such upbringing.

I have gone days without food before. Days I had to then turn to fasting and prayer not because that is what I wanted but the lack of food and money had necessitated that spiritual exercise.

I have owed bills and fees before and faced huge disgrace because of them.

I have always wanted to be financially abundant. The desire was strong and after years of searching I found the right keys to finally end my poverty and lead me into financial abundance.

Like you, I have read so many books. Self-help, spiritual, academic and what have you to cure my poverty.

I had different levels of success. The only issue was that I was not living in abundance.

Not until the February I discovered the truths you will learn in this book that I began living in financial abundance. These truths changed my whole outlook on finances.

They made me it up and sit straight. It was like a blind man who had suddenly received his sight. I began to see things I had not seen before.

That year I made other young people below 25 years rich by the revelation I gave them.

Some bought houses, some begun to send their parents money in foreign countries when months earlier it was the other way round.

Some begun to pay the fees of their siblings, a responsibility of their parents. Some begun to pay their own school fees.

The experience was humbling. Financial abundance was there for the taking and we were wallowing in lack, poverty and mediocrity.

Your own story will change. Regardless of what it is.

Say good bye to lack and welcome abundance like you have never seen before.

It is a promise I make to you. If you act on the things written in this book, your life can never be the same again.

CHAPTER ONE: BLESSED AND POOR

There once lived a man. His experience in life was like the experience of many today.

He was very blessed and very poor.

Is it possible for blessed men to be poor?

Well that is exactly what this man proved.

The blessing of God makes men rich. That is the truth of the word of God. However many men know how to deactivate the power of the blessing of God upon their lives.

Yes you read it right. They deactivate the power of the blessing of God upon their lives.

Jacob is the name of the subject of this discussion.

He worked for his uncle Laban for fourteen years. After fourteen years of hard labour, all he had was two wives and children.

He had no other property, no money and no asset to call his own. No savings to call his own. He was virtually broke. That seems a familiar story. His turnaround is even more remarkable. Let us delve deeper into the cause of his poverty.

Was he blessed?

Yes he was. Even his uncle acknowledged that fact.

> *And Laban said unto him, I pray thee, if I have found favour in thine eyes, tarry: for I have learned by experience that the LORD hath blessed me for thy sake.Genesis 30:27*

His uncle asked him to stay and continue working for him because he has seen by experience that God had blessed him for Jacob's sake.

That means Laban even knew Jacob was blessed. And Laban was in effect blessed because of Jacob.

The difference between Laban and Jacob was that Laban was rich and Jacob was very poor. Jacob was the blessed one, yet Laban was the one profiting from the blessing.

How can a blessed man be broke? It is very possible. Actually that has become the norm although it shouldn't be so in a lot of lives.

Doing something wrong?

He was blessed and broke because he was missing something.

Most Christians are broke not because God has not blessed them, it is simply because they are lacking in knowledge or revelation.

John says "you shall know the truth and the truth shall set you free".

To be free from lack and poverty we need truth.

Jacob needed truth to break free from his predicament.

Poverty and lack was not befitting of a blessed man like him. Neither is it befitting of anybody named by the name of God.

A lot of Christians are wallowing in poverty and lack and in their thinking, God has not blessed them.

For that reason, they keep bombarding God day and night with prayers when in reality most of them are not poor and in lack because of a lack of blessing.

The simple reason for that state is a lack of revelation.

If we could stop complaining and begin to ask God to open the eyes of our understanding, we will go far in life.

Every problem has a solution including the problem of lack and poverty.

The origin of a lot of the poverty people face is in their mind.

If only their minds can be renewed, their poverty can be cured.

A wise man once said "if you think you can, you are right. And if you think you cannot, you are also right"

It simply reveals the impact the mind plays in our life.

Most poor people are programmed in their minds to make poor financial decisions. They are also programmed not to recognize financial opportunities. These together with other negative programming is what leads most people into lack and poverty.

That is why anyone seeking to have financial abundance must carefully renew his or her mind.

The chapters in this book will do exactly that for anyone seriously seeking financial abundance.

The revelation in this book turned my finances and that of many others I taught around in a matter of months.

The kind of abundance they controlled is testament to the power within the revelations you will receive.

Do not be lazy about reading it. Read every chapter. You can be done reading in an hour or two and begin your pathway to financial abundance.

CHAPTER TWO: GOAL FOR WORKING

When you study the case of the man Jacob, you will realise one of the reasons he had no assets or property or money.

His goal for working was what kept him poor.

His goal for working was for a wife. He wasn't working for abundance, he was just working for a wife.

It is interesting to note that the reason for a man working for 14 years was to acquire a wife.

And for fourteen years he worked for two wives.

It is very interesting but I have come to realize that life gives you what you demand of it.

Most people are working to pay bills. Others are working to get something to eat.

The problem is that more often than not your goals more than what you are doing drive you in life.

Why are you working? What is your goal for working?

Jacob was poor because he could not see beyond a wife.

You are earning less because you cannot see beyond your current salary or income.

Can you set a bigger goal as your income? What will that goal drive you to do?

What opportunities will that goal cause you to seek out?

Blessed man Jacob was blessed but poor because of a single decision.

The decision to work for a wife.

Will you decide to work for abundance rather than what to eat?

Notice what Jacob worked for

Genesis 29:18 And Jacob loved Rachel; and said, I will serve thee seven years for Rachel thy younger daughter.

Genesis 29:19 And Laban said, It is better that I give her to thee, than that I should give her to another man: abide with me.

Genesis 29:20 And Jacob served seven years for Rachel; and they seemed unto him but a few days, for the love he had to her.

After serving his first seven years, Rachel was not given to him. Leah, her elder sister was given to him. He had to work seven more years to be able to marry Rachel.

There was no way Jacob could blame God for not having anything after 14 years.

He worked those 14 years of his life and got what he really wanted. What he wanted was a wife.

You will always get what you want in life.

A lot of us say we want certain things. In truth we do not really want them. It is just a passing desire and we can do without those things.

When you really want something and decide to go for it, as a blessed person you will overcome every opposition that comes your way till you get what you really want.

Our primary goal for working has not changed

When most of us were looking for jobs, our primary goal was to survive. For many, that goal has not changed. It is the reason many are still surviving.

Your goals and desires must first change for other things to follow suit.

Your goal must now be abundance. It will change your financial results.

A goal of $5,000 a month

Imagine you have set a goal of $5000 a month but your salary is $1,000.

A typical Christian will let their salary control them, an educated Christian in the word and finances will let their goal control them.

What the above goal means is that, even though your salary is $1,000, you have enough blessing to make the additional $4,000 by applying your time and skills elsewhere to add to the $1,000.

The financially educated Christian begins to look for ways to achieve this goal because he is blessed.

The Christian with the poverty mentality will not think this way. He will think I need God to bless me.

And he will wait for the blessing till in most cases he grows old in poverty and dies. In his mind, God did not bless him.

The financially educated Christian in the word of God creates room for the blessing to operate.

He finds opportunities for the blessing to work to make the extra $4,000.

He doesn't let his present salary control him. He lets his goals drive him.

Are you being controlled by your goals or your salary?

Create room for financial increase

We must create room for financial increase by setting financial goals. That is exactly what Jacob did later in his life to turn his finances around.

And he said, Appoint me thy wages, and I will give it. Genesis 30:28

Laban told Jacob "tell me what you want to be paid and I will pay you".

It was when Jacob determined that what he was working for was financial abundance that he started experiencing abundance.

This time around he didn't say a wife. He was specific about what he really want. Know what you want, if your job or opportunity cannot give it, add additional sources and let the blessing on your life work.

Do not let your salary control you. Set your financial goals independent of your current income level or source.

You are unto something. I guess you have started putting something on paper already.

CHAPTER THREE: DECISIONS ARE NOT PREFERENCES

Many Christians are in lack and poverty. They are not experiencing financial abundance because they have not differentiated between preferences and decisions.

Preferences and Decisions

A preference is something you will like. I will like to be rich. It is just a preference. It is weak in its ability to make things happen.

A decision however is a different proposition. It is not a passive desire, it is a definite state of mind and choice.

Such clear decisions help you to take the next step.

If you are bold enough to make a decision concerning your finances, you will have ideas and release inner abilities to help you achieve it.

The Bible says:

Habakkuk 2:2 And the LORD answered me, and said, Write the vision, and make it plain upon tables, that he may run that readeth it.

After you have made the decision, it is essential to write it down so that it will cause you and anybody who sees it to run.

Running simply means to take action.

You need to take action on your decision and writing it down helps you do that.

A man's financial life should not be left on autopilot.

Conscious decisions must be taken concerning personal finances and these decisions must be followed with strategies to achieve them.

These strategies must be followed with massive action.

When Jacob made the decision to name his wage, he took massive action towards his decision.

That is what brought him financial abundance far above the man who was 14 years ahead of him.

Massive action

A little laziness, a little folding of arms can lead to a life of poverty.

It is not enough to take a concrete decision and make plans and strategies to meet that decision. You need to add action to it. Not any ordinary action, you need to add massive action.

Love not sleep, lest thou come to poverty; open thine eyes, and thou shalt be satisfied with bread.
Proverbs 20:13

Sleep is a state of inaction. It is a state of passivity. Any man that loves sleep is preparing his way to poverty.

You cannot fold your arms and expect money to jump into your pocket. You must take action to set up such an income stream.

Action has always separated winners from losers. Are you a man of words or a man of action?

It is time to make taking massive action a part of your mind-set. Keep taking action. It will take you where you want to be in life.

Without action, you will remain where you are. In your finances, you will remain at the same level without action.

And if any man desires massive results, he must take massive action.

I see you break free from the chains of inaction and passivity and stepping into the arena of massive actions and results in Jesus name.

I decided not to waste the blessing

When I decided not to waste the blessing upon my life, I made a decision to double my monthly income. I researched and found what I could do for my decision to be a reality

I found areas where I could apply myself to make extra money. Lo and behold in my first month I found one.

I was disappointed at the financial results I got in the first month of taking action. My goal did not change. I told myself I was blessed and if ordinary people were making it in that opportunity, I could make it too.

I thus changed my approach and a few strategies and in the second month I made half my monthly income. Added to my monthly income I had increased my income by 50% in just two months.

 To cut a long story short, by the end of the year I applied myself to two more opportunities and made 5 times my full time income in one year.

It is time to make a decision on your finances. Do not allow your circumstances to control you. Decide to master your circumstances.

Manis a master of his personal circumstances unless he delegates his authority to his circumstances.

You are a master of your circumstances. Take a pen and a paper, make a decision concerning your finances and decide when to take action. After the decision, begin to take action. You are too blessed to be passive.

What decision are you making today concerning your finances? Do not wait another minute. Make a firm decision now. Most poor people won't. They will rather make excuses instead of making a decision.

The rich and abundant will. The will make a decision instead of find an excuse why they cannot make a decision now. Which of them are you?

CHAPTER FOUR: WHAT THE BLESSING DOES

I keep telling people that the ordinary man who is not born again or a Christian is even equipped to have financial abundance.

The reason is simple.

Man as a creature was designed to succeed in all he does. His success is by design.

Thus the born again man who has the added firepower of the blessing of God upon his life cannot afford to play with poverty and wallow in it. It must not even be tolerated 100 meters away from you.

A lot of people have underestimated the blessing of God.

The blessing of God however is empowerment way beyond human influence to achieve what cannot be achieved ordinarily.

The Bible puts it better:

The blessing of the LORD, it maketh rich, and he addeth no sorrow with it. Proverbs 10:22.

The blessing actually makes rich. Thus in the absence of limiting beliefs and other hindrances of thought, the blessing makes people rich. Some limiting beliefs include when people believe they are cursed. Another is when people believe the economy is so hard they cannot get capital or make it financially.

The blessing is a great empowerment. It is such great empowerment that it causes men to be the envy of nations.

When you acknowledge the blessing of God upon your life and how powerful it is, it works on your behalf.

After all the Bible says that:

According to your faith be it unto you.

Matthew 9:29b

If you walk and do things like one who knows you are so supernaturally empowered that it causes things to work exceedingly well for you, you will begin to see the results you are expecting.

Some people give up too easily on the blessing

I remember when I decided to take advantage of an opportunity because I was blessed.

The first two weeks of the opportunity were terrible.

I made no money.

I told myself I had the blessing and could not fail. I studied how to make the opportunity work and in two weeks I discovered how to make the opportunity work for me.

I didn't give up on the blessing and say the opportunity should work just because I was blessed. I got the required knowledge and wisdom to make it work.

The truth that I was blessed kept me from accepting failure. It made me press on.

To people who give up easily, the Bible says:

Cast not away therefore your confidence, which hath great recompence of reward.Heb 10:35

The blessing gaveIsaac tremendous results in a time of famine

Isaac was so blessed that in the time of famine he sowed his seed and had a hundredfold harvest.

This is a man who was so blessed, a whole nation could not compete with him.

Such was the blessing of Abraham too.

The blessing puts you at the same level of wealth as nations, not individuals.

That is why you must not think or act small.

You have God's greater blessing as a born again Christian.

Acknowledge it and make good use of it.

Genesis 26:12 Then Isaac sowed in that land, and received in the same year an hundredfold: and the LORD blessed him.

Genesis 26:13 And the man waxed great, and went forward, and grew until he became very great:

Genesis 26:14 For he had possession of flocks, and possession of herds, and great store of servants: and the Philistines envied him.

The blessing of God upon his life made him so great that a whole nation of Philistines envied him.

The blessing you carry is so powerful, it can prosper you more than your nation.

The blessing is powerful, too powerful

Believe the power of the blessing of God upon your life.

So powerful is the blessing that, when the presence of God was at the house of Obededom for three months he experienced tremendous prosperity in that period that the king had to come for the ark of the covenant.

The blessing is of such power that it can transform finances within hours.

2Samuel 6:10 So David would not remove the ark of the LORD unto him into the city of David: but David carried it aside into the house of Obededom the Gittite.

2Samuel 6:11 And the ark of the LORD continued in the house of Obededom the Gittite three months: and the LORD blessed Obededom, and all his household.

2Samuel 6:12 And it was told king David, saying, The LORD hath blessed the house of Obededom, and all that pertaineth unto him, because of the ark of God. So David went and brought up the ark of God from the house of Obededom into the city of David with gladness.

Make that confession

I am blessed with the most powerful force that creates financial abundance.

I have the blessing.

It makes me rich.

It affects everything I do.

I exceed human expectations in all I do.

You have supernatural empowerment.

CHAPTER FIVE: BLESSED OR NOT

A lot of people will not argue with you if you told them Abraham was blessed.

They will not argue about Solomon or Isaac being blessed.

Their main contention with you will be if you told them they are also blessed.

I know many people who have decided that they are cursed in life.

They have resigned to this thought pattern because of difficulties they have faced in their financial lives.

I was once in this position and I had friends to encourage this line of thinking.

It is funny that when you have the wrong mind-set, you tend to be more comfortable with people with similar mind-sets.

They suggested all sort of prayers and things to break the curse.

As you will notice by now, it was an exercise in futility.

My problem was not a curse. It was a deep seated mind-set. Call it a culture that was leading me in perpetual poverty.

And as long as I continued in that thinking things were almost not going to change.

My breakthrough hour

My breakthrough came when I discovered two great scriptures.

The first scripture has changed my life and perspective about God and how he loves me. It has brought abundant happiness in my life.

It was the breath of fresh air I needed after a lifetime of wrong thinking that had led me to further bondage than I was in.

Are you blessed or not?

Have you ever questioned yourself like that before?

What truth do you hold about your blessing status?

This is more often than not the greatest stimulant of financial abundance in the life of the born again person.

If you can understand where you are in relation to this question and understand what it means for you, you are ready to be catapulted into abundance.

I am more than convinced I am blessed. I am more than convinced you are blessed and the good news is that I have evidence to back it.

Such evidence as you will anchor the rest of your financial abundance on.

Blessed with all spiritual blessings

What would you do if you knew you were blessed with every imaginable blessing in heaven?

What would you accomplish financially if you were empowered with the most potent financial empowerment in heaven?

Well, as it stands every born again person is equipped with every imaginable blessing in heaven. It simply means there is no excuse for financial failure. How do I know? The bible says:

Ephesians 1:3 Blessed be the God and Father of our Lord Jesus Christ, who hath blessed us with all spiritual blessings in heavenly places in Christ:

God is not about to bless you. You are already blessed with all the blessings in heaven in Christ

Jesus. In Christ you are blessed with all heavenly blessings.

You are not blessed with part. You are blessed with all the spiritual blessings in heaven.

There is no other blessing in heaven you have not been blessed with.

My o my, If only we could see what God has done for us. We will stop complaining and start receiving and acknowledging.

Did you mean every blessing? Yes the Bible says every blessing. Every empowerment you need.

You are not ordinary, heaven is working on your behalf. Why are you therefore sitting down?

Apply yourself, there is abundance all over you.

People who do not even have this blessed privilege you have are making it big financially. It is time for you to arise and make impact.

Do not waste the blessing on your life.

It will be sad to possess all this and yet produce nothing significant with it.

You are blessed to be a blessing. Do not sit on your blessing. Do something with it.

Child of God you are blessed. It is good news for anybody desiring to be financially abundant.

JOIN MY FINANCIAL ABUNDANCE COACHING.

You have read this book and believe within yourself that you can achieve financial abundance. Everything within you tells you that you will make it.

All you need now is guidance to reach that destination.

You have read of the various people I have guided to achieve financial abundance in no time.

As you read, you believe my guidance can help you too.

You are right, I am willing to help you reach your financial goals.

This year I am taking on only ten people to help on a personal basis reach their financial goals.

- I will answer all your questions
- I will help you discover opportunities around you and take advantage of them
- I will draw a normal plan with you with strategies to achieve all your financial goals.
- I will then help you set your expanded financial goals and draw a workable plan to achieve it.
- I will encourage and pray for you all year through till you achieve your financial goal.
- What I did for others to achieve financial abundance, I will do same for you.

IS THE COACHING PROGRAM RIGHT FOR ME?

This program is perfect for you if you have ever said anything like;
- I want more out of life but I don't know how to go about it or what to do.
- I have goals but they are too big I don't know if I can ever reach it.
- I don't even know what I want, am confused.
- I have great ideas, but I don't know how to bring them to light.
- I know I can be financially abundant if only I know what to do.
- I give up easily and I need someone to guide me and encourage me and let me know I am on the right path.

This is an interactive coaching program that is designed to help you answer these questions and more and to help you achieve all your financial goals and dreams to enable you reach the level of financial abundance, fulfillment in life and secure a great future for your family, loved ones and the less privileged.

As soon as you join this program, you will be taught, trained and supported until your financial future is secured.

I will be there with you every step of the way, as you build, create and secure your dream life.

WHY SHOULD I JOIN?

Each time I talk to people about joining my coaching program, the first question they ask is "WHY"? In other not to leave you in the dark as to why you should enroll in this program I have decided to put down few answers to that question.

* All the people who enrolled in this program last year experienced a major turnaround in their financial life. I have built my skills of motivation, encouragement, teaching and pushing the people who enroll till they achieve their goals.

* I will not coach you simply by asking you to read books or watch YouTube videos and so on. I will join you; hold your hands as we walk together through the dark until you get to light, where you will experience financial abundance, true wealth and fulfillment. We will use all communication sources to make sure the experience is as personal as possible.

DOES THE COACH HAVE THE NECESSARY EXPERIENCE TO HELP ME?

This is another common question I get when I invite people for the program. To be honest at first it wasn't easy convincing people to enroll because I had no one to point at that I have helped and taught and helped to achieve financial abundance except myself but that is not the case now because I have people flying high at the top I can point at... I will be glad to also you get to that level of abundance so you can start flying with the aircraft of financial abundance and sailing with the ship of financial freedom.

TESTIMONIES

The testimonies you are about to read are mind blowing, but they will be nothing compared to what you will receive as soon as you enroll because I have become wiser and gained more experience.

1. Before I attended this great program, both my life and my finances were in shambles. I was a passenger on earth. But after the first day of the program I began to notice a positive change and a shift in my life. When Dr. Francis spoke, he interrupted the thoughts of failure and lack going on in my mind. He helped restore the belief in me that I could climb the ladder of success and get to the top. He helped change the program that was running in me and helped me become a conscious Creator of my future... After one month, I turned $100 into $3,000. You can read my book on Amazon titled; "SECRET TO HAVING ALL YOU

WANT" I wrote that book after he helped me find my purpose in life and helped me establish my enterprise in less than 3 months. Today am happy to recommend this program to you, it will transform your life and finances.

   - MICHAEL ENDWELL

2. After I attended the financial coaching program last year 2016, in less than 3 months I started my own business and 3 months later I bought my own house... I recommend this program to anyone who wants more out of life.

   - JAMES BARNABAS

3. Because of this financial coaching program, I was able to start my own business. Today I am very proud of where I am financially. My life would have still been a mess if not for this program. I will recommend this program to anyone especially women who want to attain financial freedom. I am a very young woman and what I have attained

financially still remains a wonder to me. There are people you meet that just have a way of making your life so much better. Dr. Francis is one of them.
 - POSH

4. What still keeps me wondering is how fast this program transformed me and my finances.
This program has turned my whole life around. Because of this Program I have moved from a struggling small business owner to one who employs people. I highly recommend this program...
   - STANLEY

After these testimonies and many more I decided to take action to help others who I feel need this transformation.
Seeing how fast this program transformed the lives of these individuals who when I met them were struggling financially, I decided that it's time for me

to help you too to reach your financial goals and attain financial abundance...

HOW DO I ENROLL?

NOTE: I am only taking ten people. This is so because I want to make the program as effective as possible. I want to ensure I have enough time to work with the ten who really want financial abundance in no time.

If you want to be part of this number that will achieve financial abundance this year, send me a mail. My email is drfrancisjonah@gmail.com. Title your mail FINANCIAL ABUNDANCE COACHING. Don't miss out.

DO I HAVE TO PAY?

There will be a small commitment fee so I can dedicate time to help you and also know your level OF seriousness about achieving your financial goals. Most people are only talk and take valuable contributions to their success for granted. It is the reason I want the best prepared people as much as possible.

For a whole year of personal coaching, you will need to commit $500.

This amount will be a token after few months of coaching because; you will make more than ten times of that amount. Some also will make a hundred and thousand times that amount as is evident from the testimonies.

TAKE ACTION NOW!

Send me an email to join this elite group that will create financial abundance in no time.

My email is **drfrancisjonah@gmail.com.** Title your mail FINANCIAL ABUNDANCE COACHING.

You know you have to make that decision now. Do not procrastinate. Send the email now.

My email is **drfrancisjonah@gmail.com**. Title your mail FINANCIAL ABUNDANCE COACHING. Abundance awaits you.

CHAPTER SIX: WASTING THE BLESSING

Many lives have become synonymous with waste.

We waste time. We waste money. We waste opportunities. We waste relationships. We waste mentors. We waste protégés. We waste water. We waste electricity.

Waste has almost become like a culture to most of us.

It is deeply rooted in our programming. It is deeply rooted in our thinking.

Most people by eliminating or reducing waste alone can create abundance for themselves.

The time you waste can be used to create financial abundance. The money you waste can be used to create financial abundance. The relationships you waste can be used to create financial abundance.

The most important thing Christians waste before we even consider time and money is the unlimited blessing of God on their lives.

Wasted time to money

I write when most people are wasting that time on television or sitting in a car or bus doing nothing.

My writing creates finances for me. The impact on lives is greater. Nonetheless it comes with financial rewards.

Wasted relationships to money

There were two people who liked me a lot. They were very loyal to me but very poor. When I discovered the truth about financial abundance I taught them and went into joint ventures with them.

These ventures have created an amazing flow of finances. These relationships were wasted some time ago but now I make lots of money from these relationships.

The list of waste converted to money is so much.

Wasted money to capital.

When I stopped eating outside and decided to eat home cooked food, I saved a sizable amount of money to buy a small asset after six months. That asset is still producing money for me.

Curbing waste has the potential to transform your finances and introduce financial abundance.

Jesus practiced avoiding waste.

> *Matthew 14:20 And they did all eat, and were filled: and they took up of the fragments that remained twelve baskets full.*

The fragments or the leftovers alone gathered was twelve baskets.

Even Jesus avoided waste because more often than not, what people waste is the source of someone else's financial breakthrough.

Recycling is a typical lesson

Most companies that recycle take what people call waste and do something profitable with it.

It is time to avoid waste if we really want to be financially abundant. Identify the waste in your life. Everybody has waste in his or her life.

Identify them and eliminate them. Keep the financial results of the eliminated waste in your life and see how it can be used in the long term into something profitable.

The main waste

The main thing Christians waste is the blessing of God.

Any Christian who is in lack and not helping others is just wasting the blessing of God upon their lives.

How can blessed men live the life of paupers?

How can a man destined to feed continents settle for poverty and lack and going from hand to mouth?

That should not be said about you.

A blessed man must of necessity apply the blessing of God upon his life to create abundance.

Do not sit down and waste all that blessing on your life. For goodness sake, we are blessed with every blessing in heaven.

You are better than sitting and watching people suffer when you have something you can use to create better lives for them.

Do not waste the blessing on your life. Do something with it. Create financial abundance with it. It is required of you.

You are not cursed, you are blessed. Blessed people cannot be cursed. I repeat, they cannot be cursed.

Galatians 3:13 Christ hath redeemed us from the curse of the law, being made a curse for us: for it is written, Cursed is every one that hangeth on a tree:

Galatians 3:14 That the blessing of Abraham might come on the Gentiles through Jesus Christ; that we might receive the promise of the Spirit through faith.

Every curse was removed whether generational or institutional for the blessing to come to you. Man, woman, you are blessed.

Do not waste it. Right now think of what you can do. Put the blessing to work.

CHAPTER SEVEN: WRONG FOCUS

Many men have channelled their energies into wrong things.

When productive time and energy is channelled into the wrong thing, these resources are very much wasted and do not bring the results they are meant to bring.

Where is your focus?

I have seen many men whose focus is on God to bless them.

They pray morning, afternoon and evening for the blessing of God.

To them they are not blessed and need to pray harder for God to bless them.

They have been praying for the past ten years for God to bless them.

If God wanted to bless them (assuming he has not) wouldn't he have blessed them in all the ten years of asking?

These people waste their energies and time praying for something they already have.

Instead of receiving it and giving the blessing the opportunity to work in their lives, they are still praying for it.

The enemy is more than happy for you to focus on the blessing which you already have rather than putting it to use.

The young man learned the lesson

I knew a young man whose daily prayer was for God to bless him. For twelve years he prayed this prayer and still saw nothing. He was living from hand to mouth and needed a way out of the situation.

When I showed him Ephesian 1:3, he said"does that mean all those years he was praying for God to bless him, he was wasting his time?"

Ephesians 1:3 Blessed be the God and Father of our Lord Jesus Christ, who hath blessed us with all spiritual blessings in heavenly places in Christ:

I asked him whether that is the meaning he got from the scripture.

He said yes. He then asked what he must do. I told him "do not waste the blessing, put it to work".

Four months later he came to me and gave me a seed. It was half of my monthly income. He then narrated how financial abundance had come his way and he had bought an acre of land to develop and how he was helping other people pay their fees.

All this in four months of exposure to the teaching you are receiving in this book.

He just could not waste the blessing.

He told me how he begun to see opportunities all around him he could apply the blessing to.

Before the teaching, his focus was not on the opportunities he could apply the blessing to. His focus was on God blessing him.

I should have met you earlier

I shared these same teachings with another young man. He was complaining bitterly about the economy.

He vowed that the day God will bless him, people will see him.

I asked him when that day was coming. His only reply was soon.

Soon had been more than 5 years and the day had not come for God to bless him. Just a month after the teaching, he brought three more friends to listen to the teaching.

They came because they couldn't understand how he was prospering after just a month. He told them I had the key.

Focus on what to do with the blessing. Stop focusing on the economy and how difficult things are.

Stop looking for people to comfort you in your poverty.

Focus on your lack of action despite the fact that you have all these blessings and do something about your finances.

CHAPTER EIGHT: MASTER KEY OF RAIN

I remember years past. I used to jump around and play when it rained.

Rain was an opportunity for children to run around naked and enjoy the soothing effect of nature's best.

To many of us, rain is just rain.

It is as meaningless as the word octagon is in the vocabulary of many of us.

The fact that it is meaningless to a lot of us explains a deep rooted cause of poverty and lack.

When a man is trained in Biblical finance, rain means everything to him or her.

When it rains he virtually sees money passing by.

I myself was amazed when I received the two revelations I am about to share.

Let us read:

Deuteronomy 28:12 The LORD shall open unto thee his good treasure, the heaven to give the rain unto thy land in his season, and to bless all the work of thine hand: and thou shalt lend unto many nations, and thou shalt not borrow.

God will open his good treasure and will do two things

1. He will send rain

2. Bless the work of your hands

These two alone will cause you to lend to nations. Lending to nations is not the same as lending to individuals.

Lending to nations means you will really be financially abundant because the financial demands of nations far outweighs the financial demands of individuals.

You must understand that only two things are contributing to this level of abundance: rain and the work of your hands being blessed.

How does rain bring financial abundance?

The basic things each man needs are food, water and air.

Of the three, rain supplies two of them.

Incidentally we pay for all the two on a daily basis. The other, air is free.

It is rain that enables plants to grow. The same plants we use as food. The same food that constitutes a large part of anyone's budget.

The thinking is thus logical to assume that anybody who invests in food will never lack. Why? Human beings will always be hungry.

Any Christian who doesn't take advantage of rain is throwing finances away.

Should everyone be a farmer?

Ideally, everyone can be a farmer. Being a farmer does not mean you are the one farming. You can own a farm to take advantage of rain.

Why waste the rain, a major part of the source of financial abundance that will cause us to lend to nations.

I know people whose backyard farms have made them sizable incomes.

Some are into livestock, others are into plants.

It is a wonder why many do not take advantage of the huge opportunities God has given to us.

A pig gives birth to six to twelve piglets. A snail can bring forth more than two hundred eggs. 50 snails can thus lay 10,000 eggs. Consider the cost of a snail and think of the fact that only 50 of them can produce 10,000 other snails. Do the maths. You will not despise farming anymore.

Three pieces of corn can bring a harvest of over 200 pieces of corn.

Anyone lacking finances must consider, what else in this world brings such multiplication.

The young farmer

A young man who calls me his father begun a pig business. He works in a big company, yet understood the principle of rain I taught.

He met with a farmer already into the pig business. He bought four pigs and made arrangements with the farmer for the pigs to be taken care of at a small fee.

8 months later he has 16 pigs. These 16 pigs can be sold at a good amount in 8 more months.

If he chooses he can keep them and multiply them again.

He has bosses that earn more than him, this decision he took to farm has changed his whole financial outlay. By his estimation in the next two years, the pigs can give him more money than he will make in 5 years.

This is a man who knows how to take advantage of natural law.

The same principle applies to those into crops. The abundance you need is already provided by God. Just take advantage of it.

I deal in food too

I have a food business whereby I send people to buy crops from villages where they are abundant and sell the produce in the city where it is scarce to make a handsome amount of money.

I have decided to start my own crop farm so I can buy my own produce at a cheaper price and sell at a profit. The rain will do the best part of the work.

My snail farm is already taking shape. The modalities have been worked out.

Financial abundance is so easy for the man that understands biblical finance. Do not be lazy in your mind, take action. You know what to do.

Poverty is not your friend. Rise up from your current financial position. You deserve better. You deserve abundance.

CHAPTER NINE: BLESSED HANDS

If you are blessed, everything about you is blessed. That means your hands are blessed.

The second thing God said will help you lend to nations was that the work of your hands shall be blessed.

> **Deuteronomy 28:12 The LORD shall open unto thee his good treasure, the heaven to give the rain unto thy land in his season, and to bless all the work of thine hand: and thou shalt lend unto many nations, and thou shalt not borrow.**

My hands are blessed

I remember clearly when I realised my hands were blessed.

I asked myself "why are you not touching anything if your hands are blessed?"

I began to think of things I could touch to bring me financial abundance.

If I told you I slept, I would be lying. My mind kept racing. It was on a race to uncover things I could touch with my blessed hands.

Asking good questions always leads to incredible breakthroughs.

I found so many opportunities after that question and started with the one I was most comfortable with.

Success didn't come in two weeks but I encouraged myself that I was blessed and whatever I touch must succeed. I went online and got knowledge and applied wisdom and finally the opportunity generated a lot of income for me.

As earlier stated, the first two weeks were really bad but I persevered. I got the required knowledge, applied it and I began my path to abundance in that opportunity.

Setbacks do not mean give up

I see many Christians give up at the least resistance. It simply shows they do not believe they are blessed.

During any form of opposition I tell myself my hands are blessed. I do not fail and I make what is not working work.

Where there is a will, they say, there is always a way.

The fact that something is not working at the moment does not mean it won't work at all.

As a blessed man or woman, you need to make it work. This is especially so when you have seen other people make it work.

When you have an example of others making it work, you have no excuse not to succeed despite the setbacks you may face.

Apply yourself to know how to make it work and it will surely work.

OPPORTUNITIES ABOUND

We live in a world that abounds with opportunities, that is why it is wrong to give up in life or when one opportunity doesn't turn out the way you want it. There are over 10 million opportunities available to you alone.

Note it very well. Not ten opportunities, not hundred opportunities, not a million opportunities but over ten million opportunities for only you to take advantage of.

Do not sit and limit yourself to one or two opportunities. Actually do not sit and even refuse to acknowledge the presence of opportunities.

Financial abundance is there for your taking. Let it not pass you by.

It is so easy to attain financial abundance it will take a lot of effort on your part not to experience it. The truth is people are working so hard not to be financially abundant.

It is so easy that people who are not even blessed have so much financial abundance. How much more you?

Your hands are blessed. It means whatever you venture into has the ability to succeed and prosper and flourish.

Do not fold those blessed hands. Do not limit the impact those blessed hands of yours can make.

Put it to work.

You are more than a conqueror. In the area of finances too, victory is yours.

You are more than equipped to make it big in that area.

I see you feed nations, I see you provide school fees and scholarships for many. I see you build and give out houses for free.

That is the life of people with blessed hands.

Two ventures at one location

I remember one person I taught this to. She had a location where she was doing nothing. Within three months of the teaching, she had set up two different income streams at that location. All along she was wasting the blessing and her blessed hands.

She is now making a good income from the two things without her presence.

When you understand that your hands are blessed or the truth that whatever you touch is blessed you just keep touching things.

There are people in need and they are looking for blessed people like you to take your place of financial abundance.

You will employ many, trust me, you will.

CHAPTER TEN: LENDING TO MANY NATIONS

I used to be the type that could not think abundance. I could not imagine myself building a whole university with my own funds and pay for the fees of every student therein.

I didn't think I could pay the fees of people, I didn't think I could help people start businesses.

This all changed when I absorbed myself in the word of God and realized the things I could do as a blessed child of God.

The more I studied the word, the more I saw what I was capable of. I would not say I am thinking at my highest potential but now my confidence of what I am capable of is higher than it used to be.

The word has trained me.

I have paid fees of several people, I have helped several others start business,I have given capital to many more.

That shows the elevation my mind and finances have received.

LEND TO NATIONS, NOT INDIVIDUALS

When I discovered that my portion was to lend to nations, I was taken aback.

When you live a life when even what you have is not enough, you wonder if you can have enough to lend to individuals.

Then you discover that your calling is to lend to nations. Nations, countries. Not one nation, but many nations.

Think of the money nations borrow. Think of the infrastructural demands and problems these amounts go to solve.

Now begin to imagine yourself signing off such cheques to the nations.

That is your express calling in terms of finances.

You are called to lend to nations. Are you walking that calling? If not, it is not a problem. Everybody started from somewhere. Just know that potential is within you and you must bring it out.

Today, make the decision to fulfil the scripture:

> *Deuteronomy 28:12 The LORD shall open unto thee his good treasure, the heaven to give the rain unto thy land in his season, and to bless all the work of thine hand: and thou shalt lend unto many nations, and thou shalt not borrow.*

I decree over your life that you will lend to many nations before your life ends in Jesus name. Not one nation, not two nations, not three nations, not ten nations but many nations.

I see that come to pass in your own life.

AVAILABLE RESOURCES

God did not give you that calling in a vacuum. He has given us all it takes to fulfil that mandate.

You are not alone. You are well equipped to lend to many nations.

You have what it takes. Never for a minute doubt how equipped you are. God has equipped you so well.

You can only limit God in your mind and what you believe. According to your faith be it unto you.

Do you believe God and his word? The good book says:

Numbers 23:19 God is not a man, that he should lie; neither the son of man, that he should repent: hath he said, and shall he not do it? or hath he spoken, and shall he not make it good?

God will not lie to you. The door to financial greatness has been opened unto you. It is not about to open. You have been equipped, you are not about to be equipped.

It is decision time, will you enter into that door?

Will you be what God has called you to be? Will you be blessed and be a blessing to your generation and generations after you?

If yes, take a book and begin to write your financial goals. After the goals put down your plans and strategy.

I recommend my two books on goal setting to help you achieve your financial goals.

And if the task looks to huge for you, remember:

EVERYBODY STARTED FROM ZERO

Though your beginning seems humble, your end shall be great.

Most people you see with substantial wealth started from zero.

They started from where you are starting from.

I remember hearing great stories of how people were so wealthy. Sometimes I wondered to myself if I would ever get there.

The truth of the matter is that most if not all of these people started from zero.

That is what I kept reminding myself of when I began the journey of financial abundance. It is the reason I kept building. I didn't get discouraged by where I was at present, I knew where I was going. Soon enough I was building abundance past where I used to be. I am not yet at lending to nations, but I am getting there fast.

THOSE I OWED NOW OWE ME

In case you are in debt, it is not a cause to worry. Stop focusing on the debt and focus on creating financial abundance to deal with the debt.

I remember I used to owe some people. They really tormented me for their money. Today they are owing me and I have not even bothered to ask them for the money. Wow. You can be so abundant that you do not even think of those that owe you.

When you start from zero or negative, very soon, you will find yourself in the positive and producing amazing financial testimonies. Just start the journey of financial abundance.

Receive grace to come out of debt and enter into financial abundance. You will have a testimony in Jesus name.

Grace is available, use it. Do not sit down, arise and shine. Today is a good day to start.

JOIN MY FINANCIAL ABUNDANCE COACHING.

You have read this book and believe within yourself that you can achieve financial abundance. Everything within you tells you that you will make it.

All you need now is guidance to reach that destination.

You have read of the various people I have guided to achieve financial abundance in no time.

As you read, you believe my guidance can help you too.

You are right, I am willing to help you reach your financial goals.

This year I am taking on only ten people to help on a personal basis reach their financial goals.

- I will answer all your questions
- I will help you discover opportunities around you and take advantage of them

- I will draw a normal plan with you with strategies to achieve all your financial goals.
- I will then help you set your expanded financial goals and draw a workable plan to achieve it.
- I will encourage and pray for you all year through till you achieve your financial goal.
- What I did for others to achieve financial abundance, I will do same for you.

IS THE COACHING PROGRAM RIGHT FOR ME?

This program is perfect for you if you have ever said anything like;

- I want more out of life but I don't know how to go about it or what to do.
- I have goals but they are too big I don't know if I can ever reach it.
- I don't even know what I want, am confused.
- I have great ideas, but I don't know how to bring them to light.
- I know I can be financially abundant if only I know what to do.

- I give up easily and I need someone to guide me and encourage me and let me know I am on the right path.

This is an interactive coaching program that is designed to help you answer these questions and more and to help you achieve all your financial goals and dreams to enable you reach the level of financial abundance, fulfillment in life and secure a great future for your family, loved ones and the less privileged.

As soon as you join this program, you will be taught, trained and supported until your financial future is secured.

I will be there with you every step of the way, as you build, create and secure your dream life.

WHY SHOULD I JOIN?

Each time I talk to people about joining my coaching program, the first question they ask is "WHY"? In other not to leave you in the dark as to

why you should enroll in this program I have decided to put down few answers to that question.

* All the people who enrolled in this program last year experienced a major turnaround in their financial life. I have built my skills of motivation, encouragement, teaching and pushing the people who enroll till they achieve their goals.

* I will not coach you simply by asking you to read books or watch YouTube videos and so on. I will join you; hold your hands as we walk together through the dark until you get to light, where you will experience financial abundance, true wealth and fulfillment. We will use all communication sources to make sure the experience is as personal as possible.

DOES THE COACH HAVE THE NECESSARY EXPERIENCE TO HELP ME?

This is another common question I get when I invite people for the program. To be honest at first it wasn't easy convincing people to enroll because I had no one to point at that I have helped and taught and helped to achieve financial abundance except myself but that is not the case now because I have people flying high at the top I can point at... I will be glad to also you get to that level of abundance so you can start flying with the aircraft of financial abundance and sailing with the ship of financial freedom.

TESTIMONIES

The testimonies you are about to read are mind blowing, but they will be nothing compared to what you will receive as soon as you enroll because I have become wiser and gained more experience.
1. Before I attended this great program, both my life and my finances were in shambles. I was a passenger on earth. But after the first day of the program I began to notice a positive change and a

shift in my life. When Dr. Francis spoke, he interrupted the thoughts of failure and lack going on in my mind. He helped restore the belief in me that I could climb the ladder of success and get to the top. He helped change the program that was running in me and helped me become a conscious Creator of my future... After one month, I turned $100 into $3,000. You can read my book on Amazon titled; "SECRET TO HAVING ALL YOU WANT" I wrote that book after he helped me find my purpose in life and helped me establish my enterprise in less than 3 months. Today am happy to recommend this program to you, it will transform your life and finances.

   - MICHAEL ENDWELL

2. After I attended the financial coaching program last year 2016, in less than 3 months I started my own business and 3 months later I bought my own house... I recommend this program to anyone who wants more out of life.

- JAMES BARNABAS

3. Because of this financial coaching program, I was able to start my own business. Today I am very proud of where I am financially. My life would have still been a mess if not for this program. I will recommend this program to anyone especially women who want to attain financial freedom. I am a very young woman and what I have attained financially still remains a wonder to me. There are people you meet that just have a way of making your life so much better. Dr. Francis is one of them.
- POSH

4. What still keeps me wondering is how fast this program transformed me and my finances.
This program has turned my whole life around. Because of this Program I have moved from a struggling small business owner to one who employs people. I highly recommend this program...

- STANLEY

After these testimonies and many more I decided to take action to help others who I feel need this transformation.

Seeing how fast this program transformed the lives of these individuals who when I met them were struggling financially, I decided that it's time for me to help you too to reach your financial goals and attain financial abundance...

HOW DO I ENROLL?

NOTE: I am only taking ten people. This is so because I want to make the program as effective as possible. I want to ensure I have enough time to work with the ten who really want financial abundance in no time.

If you want to be part of this number that will achieve financial abundance this year, send me a mail. My email is drfrancisjonah@gmail.com. Title your mail FINANCIAL ABUNDANCE COACHING.

Don't miss out.

There will be a small commitment fee so I can dedicate time to help you and also know your level OF seriousness about achieving your financial goals. Most people are only talk and take valuable contributions to their success for granted. It is the reason I want the best prepared people as much as possible.

For a whole year of personal coaching, you will need to commit $500.

This amount will be a token after few months of coaching because; you will make more than ten times of that amount. Some also will make a hundred and thousand times that amount as is evident from the testimonies.

TAKE ACTION NOW!

Send me an email to join this elite group that will create financial abundance in no time.

My email is **drfrancisjonah@gmail.com.** Title your mail FINANCIAL ABUNDANCE COACHING.

You know you have to make that decision now. Do not procrastinate. Send the email now.

My email is **drfrancisjonah@gmail.com**. Title your mail FINANCIAL ABUNDANCE COACHING. Abundance awaits you.

CHAPTER ELEVEN: UNQUANTIFIABLE POTENTIAL

One of the most amazing scriptures I have seen in my life is found in Philippians.

It is so amazing that sometimes I wonder why I operate below my capacity in life.

Let us read:

Philippians 4:13 I can do all things through Christ which strengtheneth me.

I can do all things through Christ who gives me ability.

It means I have someone who gives me ability. That ability can do all things.

I have an enabler within me who enables me to do all things I have been called to do.

Gone are the days when you hear people say I cannot do it. Today you know there is an enabler within you.

Wow. There is an enabler within me. That is powerful stuff.

EXCUSES

I have realized that when people do not want to do something, they actually find excuses.

Some people are professional excuse finders. They will find excuses for everything.

They will even find an excuse not to be financially abundant.

They will say things like I have no capital, I cannot identify any opportunity, my job is time consuming, I am not like you, I do not have helpers.

While they are busy giving the excuse, others are asking "how can I?"

The "how can I?" group are achievers. They are not excuse makers. They make things happen.

Excuse makers find a way of wasting their potential and the life God called them to.

If you are an excuse maker, it is time to renew your mind. That is not your calling. Excuse making is so cheap and unworthy of you.

Such small margins are the differences between the financially abundant and those who live from pay check to pay check.

SETTLE IT IN YOUR MIND

You do not lack ability. You need to settle it in your mind and heart.

Whatever it is that God has called you to, you have the ability to fulfil it. That certainly includes financial abundance.

You are called to be a blessing. That ability is within you.

You are called to be financially abundant, that ability is within you.

You are called to lend to nations: that ability is within you.

You are called to heal, that ability is within you.

You are called to prosper and be in health: that ability is within you.

You have so much ability, you can be the envy of your generation if you decide to put it to work.

Your problem is not the lack of ability.

Your problem is that you have not decided to tap into the power within you and use it for the benefit of all the people around you.

SELFLESSNESS

It is time to be selfless. You need to stop thinking only about yourself.

When you think of others, you do more.

Whatever is in you is not for you alone, it is for the people around you.

Jesus said it well:

Matthew 23:11 But he that is greatest among you shall be your servant.

He said the greatest will be the one that serves.

The one who uses his or her ability to the benefit of others.

I have come to realise that the richest people are the people who affect and serve the many.

Are you ready to serve the many with your ability?

Selfless people attain greatness. They think about the many rather than themselves.

Selfish people are always thinking about themselves. Such thinking does not take men far.

It is time to think of others and put the ability within you to work.

There is unlimited ability to do all things in you. It will marvel the world what you can and will achieve.

Think of the sick and dying, the poor, needy and helpless. They need you. Do not add to the number. Do not add to the problem, be a solution in your own way. Break free from lack and enter into abundance. Not for your sake, but for the sake of others.

THE RICHEST SERVE THE MULTITUDES

Think of Bill Gates, Ali Dangote, Mark Zuckerberg, Jeff Bezos and other rich people. One thing you will find in common amongst them is that they serve the many.

Facebook, Microsoft, amazon are all serving the many, no wonder they are so rich.

It is high time you begin to think that way. How do I serve the multitudes?

It is time to serve the multitudes. There is something in you. The world as a stage awaits your entrance.

You are great. You are filled with unlimited potential. I feel it right now as I write.

You can do something. You can impact our world.

CHAPTER TWELVE: POWER TO MAKE WEALTH

I told a man the other day that he determines what he earns.

If he earns little, he determines it and if he earns much he determines it.

He looked at me in awe and turned away with that little wisdom I imparted. He may not have understood it immediately, but I know he finally will.

THE THEORY OF ACRES

Did you know that all things being equal, if I plant on 5 acres and another person plants on 1 acre, I will produce more harvest than the person?

It is the same way with wealth. You can determine how wealthy you are.

The scripture reveals it in a special way. It says:

Deuteronomy 8:18 But thou shalt remember the LORD thy God: for it is he that giveth thee power to get wealth, that he may establish his covenant which he sware unto thy fathers, as it is this day.

What God does for us is that He gives us power to make wealth.

What you do with that power is solely up to you.

Do you mean I have power to make wealth? Rightly so. It is documented truth.

YOU HAVE POWER TO MAKE WEALTH

If you and me have power to make wealth. The first question is "are we aware we have power to make wealth?"

Most people are not aware that they have power to make wealth. It is the reason they go round seeking that power.

There is a special anointing and power to make wealth and God is saying He has given you that power.

You need to believe it and know it.

You need to confess it to yourself. "I have the special power to make wealth". God has given you that power freely.

He loves you and wants you to succeed.

He has given you the most important and most expensive and most priceless thing he has. Jesus.

That is why the power to make wealth is so easy for him to give. He already gave you the most expensive and costly thing for free. The less valuable things are thus a bonus.

He states it like this:

Romans 8:32 He that spared not his own Son, but delivered him up for us all, how shall he not with him also freely give us all things?

Awesome. You are so full of wealth producing power. What are you doing with that power? Is it being used to make impact or you are allowing it to rot away?

I know men and women begging for such power. You have it by birth. You have it because you believe in Jesus Christ. You have it because you are born again.

Can you please put that power to work? It is sad to see such power waste away in your life.

It is power many are killing for and travelling nations for and making all sorts of sacrifices for.

You have it. If only we will realise how great that power within us is. We will take the world by storm.

There is something about you that others do not have or cannot understand. You are special and equipped.

STOP CHASING USELESS THINGS AND PUT THE POWER TO WORK

Many people are chasing miracles when they are the miracles waiting to happen.

Many are chasing power when the power to make wealth is sitting right within them.

Many are chasing prayers when the power to make things happen is sitting right within them.

It is an exercise in futility when you are chasing something you already have.

What you need to do is to be putting that power to work.

I see you break free from your old thinking and moving towards financial abundance in Jesus name.

There is so much abundance around us that you need to stop seeing the lack and start recognizing the abundance.

The world is waiting for your manifestation.

Bibles must be distributed, the poor must be fed, churches must be built, missionaries must be sent, the sick must be taken care of, the naked must be clothed, the homeless must be sheltered.

What are you waiting for? Do you not still believe you are needed in this world? Your impact is greatly needed. Quit sitting and fulfil your calling.

The power to do that has been given unto you.

You are an agent of financial abundance sent by God. You have been equipped to make great impact financially.

Will you arise and shine and take your place? There is a rallying call for mighty men and women of wealth. Will you answer the call? The world needs you.

I love how the Bible puts it:

Isaiah 60:1 Arise, shine; for thy light is come, and the glory of the LORD is risen upon thee.

It is time for you to arise, revelation has come to you. Shine, make impact. You are blessed and have special power to make wealth.

CHAPTER THIRTEEN: SEEDTIME AND HARVEST

There is a blessing the earth is blessed with. The blessing of seed time and harvest.

Many men and women have used this blessing to make so much in life. They have created exceedingly great abundance because of this blessing available to all.

Genesis 8:22 While the earth remaineth, seedtime and harvest, and cold and heat, and summer and winter, and day and night shall not cease.

They have created so much abundance with this blessing of seed time and harvest that I am sure they are asking why people do not recognize this blessing.

The power of seed time and harvest is so great that it is marvellous the results it produces. There are many forms of seeds apart from farming seeds.

But you see the importance of farming here again.

You plant corn and you get over one hundred times what you planted.

That is the power of seed time and harvest. I will keep encouraging every believer to try some form of farming.

Farming best uses the principle and blessing of seed time and harvest.

Seed time and harvest is so great that it is what made Abraham, Isaac and Jacob mighty men of wealth.

Imagine those who even rear and sell puppies. The puppies give birth to more than six at a time. Harvest at its best.

DO YOU RECOGNIZE SEED TIME?

Have you ever realised the blessing of seed time and harvest at work since you began to desire financial abundance?

I am not talking about mere observation but a conscious awakening of the work of God in motion.

Are you aware of the great multiplication seeds go through during harvest?

Have you seen a single mango seed become a tree and produce over a thousand mango fruits in its lifetime?

This is a wonderful phenomenon. Why not take advantage of it.

Again I ask "why"

DECIDE TO TAKE ADVANTAGE OF SEED TIME AND HARVEST

More often than not, a single decision is all it takes to start the journey of financial abundance.

One such decision is to decide to take advantage of seed time and harvest.

It is so simple to take such a decision and begin to work at it.

If you really want to be financially abundant, this is not the time to make excuses.

Make the decision and take massive action to bring the decision to pass.

More often than not people say they want to be financially abundant. The truth is that many people do not mean it. If they meant it, financial abundance will be easy for them.

Why? They will do the easy things people find so difficult to do.

They will take action every step of the way. Truly there is no secret to financial abundance only people who are not hungry enough to apply the truths of financial abundance.

YOUR MONEY IS ALSO A SEED

Your money can be a seed. It all depends on you.

You can either sow it like a seed to bring future results or spend it to bring present satisfaction.

It is better to go hungry and have seed than to be full and have no seed.

Your seed secures your future. When your future is abundant, you will forget your present difficulties.

You are never too broke to keep seed.

Your money is not so small that you cannot leave a portion as seed.

It is wisdom.

You must always have seed. That is what will make the difference in your life.

Another wonderful story

Your money can multiply. I remember a young man I taught this to.

He saved a part of his little income as seed till it was enough to buy an animal. It took him six months to save the money.

That seed was used to buy an animal that produced so many offspring. He will sell them and harvest from the seed he kept despite his small income.

He said the decision was difficult nut once he made the decision, he is glad he did.

In his own words, he already feels financially abundant. He has broken a major barrier. He has taken advantage of seed time and harvest.

Some people know how to change their financial fortunes. What looks like a little step eventually leads many to financial abundance.

The proceeds of his animal sales could be seed for more animals which will produce more harvest.

He will well be on his way to great riches after sowing the third or fourth time.

Seed time and harvest are a great blessing. I wouldn't pass that opportunity. Neither should you.

Will you take advantage of seed time and harvest or you will let another great blessing pass you by. The choice is yours. My advice is for you to do all you can to take advantage of seed time and harvest.

CHAPTER FOURTEEN: SLACKING

Do not die of thirst where there is abundance of water.

Look around you. Look at the world we live in. You will see a display of wealth and abundance.

You know it, I know it. You have a deep belief that your abundance is also out there. You cannot imagine that lack and poverty is all the world has to offer you.

This is not a mere belief. It is something you know. There is more out there for you.

The important question is that why are you not getting your portion?

If you have read every chapter till now, I am confident you have a renewed mind concerning financial abundance.

The issue now is slackness. Refusal to take action or giving up when you should know that blessed people do not fail.

POSSESS YOUR POSSESSIONS

Why would a man need to possess his possessions? Well, the fact that something is yours does not mean that you are enjoying it.

Typical example is that I offer my watch for sale and get a buyer for it. I make a fine profit or some income from the watch.

The money is now mine. I exchanged a watch for it. The money had always been mine, I just didn't know how to go for it. Until I discovered I could exchange a watch for that money, I would still be without the money.

There is abundance, you need to go for it. Stop slacking and go for what belongs to you. The world is not waiting for you. That is why you need to take action now.

TYPICAL EXAMPLE OF SLACKING

Joshua 18:1 And the whole congregation of the children of Israel assembled together at Shiloh, and set up the tabernacle of the congregation there. And the land was subdued before them.

Joshua 18:2 And there remained among the children of Israel seven tribes, which had not yet received their inheritance.

Joshua 18:3 And Joshua said unto the children of Israel, How long *are* ye slack to go to possess the land, which the LORD God of your fathers hath given you?

Seven out of twelve tribes had not possessed their possessions. Five had possessed their possessions.

All the twelve had been given possessions. Five had decided to possess and did just that. The other seven is a story for another day.

The only reason they had not received their inheritance is that although they had been given, they did not want to go and possess it.

This the financial story of many people. They have been given abundance. They just are too slack, lazy or indifferent to possess it.

How else can the blessing that makes rich be stopped? Many have stopped the blessing from working spectacularly in their lives and they are still blaming God.

THEY SEE THINGS TOO FAR

Some people know what to do. They see it done.

In their minds however what needs to be done looks like a herculean task to them. Even before they begin, they have already failed in their minds.

Thus they will do nothing or stop at the least opposition to what they finally begin.

Break that barrier in your mind and develop a strong winning mentality.

Mental laziness is a killer of dreams and visions especially dreams of financial abundance.

Nothing should be too difficult in your mind. That thought of difficulty must be arrested in your mind.

To win, you must win in your mind first.

Proverbs 23:7 For as he thinketh in his heart, so *is* he.

As a man thinketh so is he. As you think, so are you.

Our major battles in life are battles of the mind.

Start winning from there. Overcome negative and limiting thoughts and take control of your financial destiny.

Overcome slackness, do something, lest you do nothing.

CHAPTER FIFTEEN: TIME AND CHANCE

Time and chance. Properly represented as time and opportunity are two significant things when it comes to achieving financial abundance.

We all have access to twenty four hours. Nobody has more than the other. We are all blessed with the same amount of time each.

Each and every day. We all have an equal twenty four hours.

For some, every hour that passes they are making millions. For others, the passing of time is just another event.

If we all have twenty four hours, we need to think carefully about what we make every hour.

Is there a way to make your time more valuable?

Is there a way to earn more per hour? Is there a way to earn even when you are asleep? The obvious answer is yes.

These are question anyone serious about financial abundance needs to ask him or herself and take serious decisions concerning them.

Ecclesiastes 9:11 I returned, and saw under the sun, that the race is not to the swift, nor the battle to the strong, neither yet bread to the wise, nor yet riches to men of understanding, nor yet favour to men of skill; but time and chance happeneth to them all.

TIME AND CHANCE HAPPENS TO ALL

Isn't it interesting that the Bible says we all have the same time and opportunities?

The opportunities people are taking advantage of are not exclusive to them. The truth of the matter is that you can also have access to those opportunities.

Many a time, we see those who are financially abundant as super human. They are not.

They are just ordinary people who had the right mind-set and took advantage of opportunities available to us all.

They invested the time we all have into that opportunity and became financially abundant.

If you think about it critically, you will realise that what makes people financially abundant is not their high IQ. It is not the capital they have access to. It is not even how long they work.

It is how they use time and opportunity.

Time and opportunity is something we all have access to. They are equalizers. If you do not take advantage of them and someone does, you have no one to blame.

People have become experts in the blame game. They blame the government, they blame their bosses, and they blame everyone and everything.

And while they do this, people are busily taking advantage of opportunities around.

Opportunities the blamers are so busy blaming, they cannot see.

STOP THE EXCUSUES

Solomon, the richest man of his time said that all the things we attribute to people being successful are not true.

The race is not to the swift. The people who win races are not the fastest in the world. They happen to have invested their time properly and discovered the sport of running as a good opportunity to exploit.

Riches is not to men of understanding. It is not their high IQ that is making them money. They invested their time into opportunities that made them money.

A lot of people have one excuse or the other why they are not financially abundant.

Can you stop the excuses and know that time and opportunities abound around you?

If you keep finding excuses, you will never find solutions.

Take that excuse mentality out of the way. You are far better than an excuse maker. You are a solution to the world.

OPPORTUNITY IS A DIFFERENCE MAKER

There is something that we must all acknowledge concerning opportunities.

A good opportunity can change a man's financial situation in one day. It is the reason people must be opportunity minded instead of job minded.

Yes you can keep your job, but it doesn't stop you from finding good opportunities to pursue. At a point I had part time opportunities that were making me three times my full time income.

Those opportunities revolutionised my financial life.

Time and chance indeed happen to us all. Until the teachings you are receiving now, I was still managing my little full time income.

Many people have become managers when they were never called to manage. They were called to be abundant.

The life of management is not your life. You were called to abundance.

STOP THE MANAGING MENTALITY AND THINK ABUNDANCE

Most people are always thinking about how to manage their pay checks. That is limiting thinking.

You should be thinking how to double your income a month.

After that goal is reached, you should be thinking how to triple or quadruple that income. Not for yourself but to help others.

For myself, I am okay financially. What I earn, I earn to help others. To lend to nations

My goal right now is to make ten times the amount I make a month.

Ten times might seem big to many. The truth is that after six days of deciding that goal I have found a way of making ten times what I make a month. I am working hard at it.

For some of you, you may not reach such a goal in a month. It may take you several months or years but you will get there.

You will realise that your life is better off because of that goal.

Stop the management mentality and know that there is abundance out there for you to take your portion.

Rise up and set your goal, there is an opportunity out there waiting for you.

I am 100% sure of that.

It worked for me. It can work for you regardless of where you are in the world.

DIFFERENT OPPORTUNITIES PRODUCE DIFFERENT LEVELS OF ABUNDANCE

Some opportunities can make you ten extra dollars a day. Others can make you $100 extra a day.

There are yet others that can make you $1,000 extra a day.

Some of these opportunities can make you money whiles you sleep.

As I write, there are opportunities that are making people $10,000 a day in extra income.

These opportunities are there. Many of them, you have passed by them without recognizing them. Let us not repeat the mistakes of the past. Opportunities are begging to be taken. Please take them.

The problem is not that there is a lack of opportunity.

Some are trained to think there is lack and settle for the least in the world.

There is abundance out there. Think that way.

Do not settle for less than you are capable of. Look for the opportunities. It is those who seek that find.

I decree that you will find several opportunities that will usher you into abundance. In Jesus name.

You may start from an opportunity that brings an extra dollar but it is a good start. You will keep increasing.

As you increase you will be confident in growing your finances by larger figures.

WHEN YOU FIND A GOOD OPPORTUNITY, MONEY WILL CHASE YOU

Most people cry that they do not have capital when what they should be doing is looking for outrageously good opportunities.

I have never lacked capital before after discovering these teachings.

My opportunities are so good that people give me money to enjoy some of the benefits of the opportunity.

Imagine this.

If I come to you and tell you that I have an opportunity that gives $300 profit a day and all I need is $3000 to pursue it.

I will give you $100 profit a day if you can bring that amount of capital. If you have that money, will you give me or not?

That is how I have always presented my opportunities and I have not disappointed my investors to date. It is the way I always get capital. And because I am trustworthy and payback, I always have a long line of people ready to invest with me.

Sometimes there are setbacks but I have met the terms most of the time till I gather enough capital to pursue the opportunities alone.

Get ready for something massive. Opportunity knocks. Grab it.

JOIN MY FINANCIAL ABUNDANCE COACHING.

You have read this book and believe within yourself that you can achieve financial abundance. Everything within you tells you that you will make it.

All you need now is guidance to reach that destination.

You have read of the various people I have guided to achieve financial abundance in no time.

As you read, you believe my guidance can help you too.

You are right, I am willing to help you reach your financial goals.

This year I am taking on only ten people to help on a personal basis reach their financial goals.

- I will answer all your questions
- I will help you discover opportunities around you and take advantage of them

- I will draw a normal plan with you with strategies to achieve all your financial goals.
- I will then help you set your expanded financial goals and draw a workable plan to achieve it.
- I will encourage and pray for you all year through till you achieve your financial goal.
- What I did for others to achieve financial abundance, I will do same for you.

IS THE COACHING PROGRAM RIGHT FOR ME?

This program is perfect for you if you have ever said anything like;

- I want more out of life but I don't know how to go about it or what to do.

- I have goals but they are too big I don't know if I can ever reach it.

- I don't even know what I want, am confused.

- I have great ideas, but I don't know how to bring them to light.

- I know I can be financially abundant if only I know what to do.

- I give up easily and I need someone to guide me and encourage me and let me know I am on the right path.

This is an interactive coaching program that is designed to help you answer these questions and more and to help you achieve all your financial goals and dreams to enable you reach the level of financial abundance, fulfillment in life and secure a great future for your family, loved ones and the less privileged.
As soon as you join this program, you will be taught, trained and supported until your financial future is secured.
I will be there with you every step of the way, as you build, create and secure your dream life.

WHY SHOULD I JOIN?
Each time I talk to people about joining my coaching program, the first question they ask is "WHY"? In other not to leave you in the dark as to

why you should enroll in this program I have decided to put down few answers to that question.

* All the people who enrolled in this program last year experienced a major turnaround in their financial life. I have built my skills of motivation, encouragement, teaching and pushing the people who enroll till they achieve their goals.

* I will not coach you simply by asking you to read books or watch YouTube videos and so on. I will join you; hold your hands as we walk together through the dark until you get to light, where you will experience financial abundance, true wealth and fulfillment. We will use all communication sources to make sure the experience is as personal as possible.

DOES THE COACH HAVE THE NECESSARY EXPERIENCE TO HELP ME?

This is another common question I get when I invite people for the program. To be honest at first it wasn't easy convincing people to enroll because I had no one to point at that I have helped and taught and helped to achieve financial abundance except myself but that is not the case now because I have people flying high at the top I can point at... I will be glad to also you get to that level of abundance so you can start flying with the aircraft of financial abundance and sailing with the ship of financial freedom.

TESTIMONIES

The testimonies you are about to read are mind blowing, but they will be nothing compared to what you will receive as soon as you enroll because I have become wiser and gained more experience.
1. Before I attended this great program, both my life and my finances were in shambles. I was a passenger on earth. But after the first day of the program I began to notice a positive change and a

shift in my life. When Dr. Francis spoke, he interrupted the thoughts of failure and lack going on in my mind. He helped restore the belief in me that I could climb the ladder of success and get to the top. He helped change the program that was running in me and helped me become a conscious Creator of my future... After one month, I turned $100 into $3,000. You can read my book on Amazon titled; "SECRET TO HAVING ALL YOU WANT" I wrote that book after he helped me find my purpose in life and helped me establish my enterprise in less than 3 months. Today am happy to recommend this program to you, it will transform your life and finances.
    - MICHAEL ENDWELL

2. After I attended the financial coaching program last year 2016, in less than 3 months I started my own business and 3 months later I bought my own house... I recommend this program to anyone who wants more out of life.

- JAMES BARNABAS

3. Because of this financial coaching program, I was able to start my own business. Today I am very proud of where I am financially. My life would have still been a mess if not for this program. I will recommend this program to anyone especially women who want to attain financial freedom. I am a very young woman and what I have attained financially still remains a wonder to me. There are people you meet that just have a way of making your life so much better. Dr. Francis is one of them.
 - POSH

4. What still keeps me wondering is how fast this program transformed me and my finances.
This program has turned my whole life around. Because of this Program I have moved from a struggling small business owner to one who employs people. I highly recommend this program...

- STANLEY

After these testimonies and many more I decided
to take action to help others who I feel need this
transformation.

Seeing how fast this program transformed the lives
of these individuals who when I met them were
struggling financially, I decided that it's time for me
to help you too to reach your financial goals and
attain financial abundance...

HOW DO I ENROLL?

NOTE: I am only taking ten people. This is so
because I want to make the program as effective as
possible. I want to ensure I have enough time to
work with the ten who really want financial
abundance in no time.

If you want to be part of this number that will
achieve financial abundance this year, send me a
mail. My email is drfrancisjonah@gmail.com. Title
your mail FINANCIAL ABUNDANCE COACHING.

Don't miss out.

There will be a small commitment fee so I can dedicate time to help you and also know your level OF seriousness about achieving your financial goals. Most people are only talk and take valuable contributions to their success for granted. It is the reason I want the best prepared people as much as possible.

For a whole year of personal coaching, you will need to commit $500.

This amount will be a token after few months of coaching because; you will make more than ten times of that amount. Some also will make a hundred and thousand times that amount as is evident from the testimonies.

TAKE ACTION NOW!

Send me an email to join this elite group that will create financial abundance in no time.

My email is **drfrancisjonah@gmail.com.** Title your mail FINANCIAL ABUNDANCE COACHING.

You know you have to make that decision now. Do not procrastinate. Send the email now.

My email is **drfrancisjonah@gmail.com**. Title your mail FINANCIAL ABUNDANCE COACHING. Abundance awaits you.

CHAPTER SIXTEEN: EATERS AND SOWERS

When it comes to financial abundance, there are two kinds of people. There are the eaters and there are the sowers.

What they do is based on who they are. The eaters eat and the sowers sow.

Isaiah 55:10 For as the rain cometh down, and the snow from heaven, and returneth not thither, but watereth the earth, and maketh it bring forth and bud, that it may give seed to the sower, and bread to the eater:

EATERS

Eaters are great people. What prevents them from being financially abundant is simple.

They see whatever comes their way as something that must be consumed.

When they receive money, they see it as something that must be spent. Either carelessly or carefully, they are designed to spend.

Whatever comes their way must be consumed. Not only must it be consumed but what it must be consumed on must not be profitable in financial terms.

Eaters spend on what is popularly termedliabilities. A liability is anything that takes money out of your pocket.

Eaters buy things like big televisions that go a long way to contribute to electric bills.

They buy cars that contribute to their fuel bills.

All the things they buy are good. But one would have thought they will buy an asset first before these liabilities.

An asset is anything that puts money in your pocket. There are many things that can put money in a man's pocket.

Typical example is someone buys a big television. Another person uses that same amount to buy an oven to bake pastries and sell.

While the television is taking money out of the pocket, the oven is putting money in the pocket of the one baking and selling pastries.

With the same money for television, someone can buy animals to keep and sell at a profit.

The eater only thinks about consuming. With that mind-set, they are always buying things that will keep them poorer.

THE BAKERY THAT MADE A DIFFERENCE

A friend of mine, who we will call an eater bought a phone with an amount of money. I used that same amount of money to set up a bakery.

That bakery has made so much money over the years while the phone is likely spoilt by now.

That is a typical example of buying an asset and buying a liability.

While the asset is putting money in someone's pocket, the liability is taking money from another person's pocket.

SOWERS

Sowers are pretty much the opposite of eaters. They know whatever they get is a seed that can produce a greater harvest.

It is because of such a mind-set that they become financially abundant in no time.

They seem to know how to take advantage of seed time and harvest.

They know that it is not everything that must be consumed. They know they need seed to succeed.

When they receive money, they see it as a seed. They ask themselves where they can sow or invest this money to get better returns.

The returns are what they see as a harvest. By getting an opportunity that increases their money, they keep doing that until they are so financially abundant they cannot help but help others with their excess.

The good thing is that sowers keep looking for opportunities to increase their harvest.

Their goal is the harvest. They know some soil or opportunities can give you 30% on your seed, they know others can give 60% and others still 100%. Even though they eat some of what they receive, they keep some as seed.

THE RUDEST SHOCK OF MY LIFE

I was happily enjoying 50% returns a week on some money I had invested in a business.

I told myself that there was still an opportunity for higher returns with less investment. I told myself that the only problem was that I had not discovered that opportunity.

Lo and behold as I searched I found an opportunity that gave more than 100% on the money used. The risk was higher but I knew how to manage the risk.

I paused on that opportunity and I am about to begin again, but the truth of the matter is that I made so much money with that opportunity starting with as little as $200.

There are possibilities out there. Truth is, there are opportunities that can give 10,000% in a year (farming is a typical area, though the type of plant or animal determines the earnings).

Opportunities that can increase your investment (seed), no matter how little by 100 times or more.

ANOTHER STORY

There was a young man I gave $100 to pursue an opportunity.

To some it looks small. But with guidance and the right opportunity, no amount is too small.

Within six months he had become financially abundant. He didn't spend the money. He knew what opportunity to invest it in.

The opportunity multiplied his money several times.

Mentally lazy people will always close their mind to opportunity.

Those who are serious about financial abundance will know that even now, they possess seed.

Be a sower and not an eater because opportunities to sow and make great returns abound.

CHAPTER SEVENTEEN: MIND BARRIERS

What you cannot see yourself achieving in your mind, you will almost not achieve it in reality.

Many people before they start anything in life have already failed in their minds.

Some also generally see things as too difficult before they even start. Such thinking cripples them in life.

Proverbs 23:7 For as he thinketh in his heart, so *is* he:

NO MAN CAN RISE BEYOND HIS THINKING

There is no person on earth who can rise above his or her level of thinking.

If you think you are poor, you can never arise above that thinking.

If you think you are a failure, you can never rise beyond that thinking.

If you think you cannot make it, you cannot rise beyond that thought pattern.

For any person to rise to where they belong in life, they must renew their minds.

We are transformed by the renewal of our minds.

Romans 12:2 And be not conformed to this world: but be ye transformed by the renewing of your mind, that ye may prove what *is* that good, and acceptable, and perfect, will of God.

Your prayer doesn't bring transformation to you. It is the renewal of your mind that brings transformation.

Get to it. Let the word of God give you an abundance mentality.

If you begin to break the barrier of lack in your mind, you will break it in reality. If you break the barrier of poverty and failure in your mind, you will break it in reality. If you break the barrier of laziness in your mind, you will break it in reality.

HOW DO YOU BREAK THE BARRIER?

Barriers of the mind are broken when you stop thinking your own thoughts and find out what God is thinking concerning you.

God says you are great. That is how you must think too.

You thought you were a "nobody". That thinking has limited you up until now. Now God says you are a great man. Begin to think that way and you will break the barrier of small thinking.

God says you are rich, stop thinking you are poor. Begin to think how God says you are and soon you will act like one and attract the things rich men attract.

2Corinthians 8:9 For ye know the grace of our Lord Jesus Christ, that, though he was rich, yet for your sakes he became poor, that ye through his poverty might be rich.

Jesus became poor so you will become rich. God doesn't intend for you to be poor. No! Jesus became poor to pay the price for you to become rich.

Stop thinking your poverty or lack is honouring God. It is not. There are bigger things planned for you. You are to lend to nations. That is your calling.

Rich men give. Rich men discover opportunities. Rich men invest. Rich men do not waste. Rich men organise capital to pursue opportunities. Rich men do not give up. Rich men see problems as opportunities.

Break that mental barrier.

NOTHING IS TOO DIFFICULT. ALL THINGS ARE POSSIBLE.

I have been in situations where what people have achieved seemed so impossible to me.

All I could think about was how long it will take me, the effort involved and the skills involved. It did not take long for me to give up on pursuing those dreams.

The reason was simple. In my mind it was too huge a task.

When I considered when I was starting and what theopportunityrequired, it was obvious I could not contain or achieve it. I was so wrong.

I had made the thing difficult in my mind. That difficulty in my mind caused me not to take action.

Can you imagine the number of things not achieved because in our minds it looked beyond us?

Even God can only act based on our level of thinking. When you think small, you limit God.

Ephesians 3:20 Now unto him that is able to do exceeding abundantly above all that we ask or think, according to the power that worketh in us,

God does above our asking or thinking. It tells you that what you ask or think plays a role in what even God who is capable of all things can achieve in your life.

I pray to God that concerning your area of finances you will begin to think big. Far bigger than you are thinking now.

THINK BILLIONAIRE. MILLIONAIRE IS TOO SMALL

As you read, I am aware some of us cannot even think of becoming millionaires.

To think of becoming a billionaire is even out of question.

The truth is what really prevents you from thinking you can become a billionaire?

I ask again,

What really prevents you from thinking you can become a billionaire?

Thoughts are free yet it is difficult for people to think big.

Today liberate your thought life and dream. When you are dreaming, dream big.

DREAM BIG

Thoughts are free. Dreams are free. What is preventing you from thinking that even at this age of 70 years I can become a millionaire.

It is not strange. It has been done before.

Nothing stops you from thinking I can become a billionaire. It is more than possible. Just conceive the thought and feed it.

You are only an opportunity away from millionaire and billionaire status.

God is looking for an available person who can have such thoughts to elevate you to that level of billionaire.

I see you receive revelation that will reveal that opportunity to you in Jesus mighty name.

Thoughts are free, think great thoughts. As a man thinketh, so is he.

Think it, you are what you think.

CHAPTER EIGHTEEN: CAPITAL

I do not have capital. I do not have capital. This is the national anthem of a lot of people.

They seem to make their lack of capital their excuse for lack and poverty.

The truth of the matter is that if capital were so easy to get, there will be no poor people.

Getting capital requires the x-factor.

On the other hand getting capital is easy for those who know how to get capital.

I have never lacked capital in my life. Actually, for certain opportunities, I have had more than necessary capital, I had to reject some.

Matthew 13:12 For whosoever hath, to him shall be given, and he shall have more abundance: but whosoever hath not, from him shall be taken away even that he hath.

It was not always like that. I used to be rejected wherever I sought for capital.

When I renewed my mind, and started seeing better opportunities and reducing the risk of investors, I begun to attract great amounts and make equally great amounts in profit.

Psalm 110:3 Thy people shall be willing in the day of thy power

In the day of your power, your people will be willing. That day is now. If you can renew your mind and begin to walk in what God has made you, people will be willing to follow.

People love to follow those who bring results. Your going round telling people you are poor and need money will not make anybody follow you. Rather go round telling people you have the best opportunity in the world.

It is in the day of your power that your people will follow. Not your day of lack or your day of sorrow.

You have learned a lot in this book to start producing results. When people see results they will trust you with their capital.

People do not give capital to the poor, they give it to the rich. Why? They want their money to be safe.

CAPITAL FOLLOWS GOOD OPPORTUNITIES

I have always maintained that if you have a good deal or opportunity, you will have money chasing you. The opposite is true. A bad deal will have you chasing money.

I remember advertising an opportunity in the classifieds of a newspaper. The opportunity was so good that people had to be rejected from presenting their money to partake in the opportunity.

If the deal is not good enough, it will be hard to attract capital. If it is good enough capital will chase you.

You will notice that I advertised an opportunity in a newspaper. I did that for a small amount but I achieved great results in the exposure it got me. I reached more than five thousand people. I rejected over 30 people who wanted to partake in the opportunity.

PEOPLE GIVE UP TOO SOON

Some people give up on their search for capital after asking three people. You will notice that when I wanted to pursue one of my opportunities,I reached over 5,000 people through the media and got outstanding results. That number could even be fifty thousand people reached.

I know people who personally spoke to over 100 people before raising capital for their vision. That should tell us that we cannot give up after talking to ten people.

Winners do not quit. You must be financially abundant. Do not give up midway. You will get there.

CAPITAL MACHINE

There was a time I needed a huge amount of money. I had time but the money was not forthcoming.

I therefore gathered 10 people who could help provide the capital. Within ten months and a specified monthly contribution, we were able to raise the required capital.

10 people x 10 months x $100 = $10,000

In ten months, 10 people contributing $100 a month can help you raise ten thousand dollars.

Use this same model to raise your own amount of capital.

The people can be less or more, the time can be less or more and the money can be less or more.

The settings of the machine are variable and depend on you.

NETWORK OF FRIENDS AND FAMILY

Your family and friends are a great source of capital.

It depends on how you seek capital from them.

Once I sought capital from family, friends and church members.

I wrote a letter outlining my vision and how much I needed to fulfil that vision.

I gave about 50 people envelopes containing the letter of the vision and asking for their financial help.

The results astonished me.

Some gave very little. Others gave 100 times what most people gave.

The long and short of it is that I was able to raise capital by that method.

SAVINGS

Any man that does not have savings wants to die in poverty. **Whenever you hear someone say "I cannot save because the money I earn is not enough", it is the poverty mentality speaking.**

Actually, I save because the money I earn is not enough. This is so that my savings can become capital to take me out of that situation of poverty and lack.

If you do not have enough or earn enough, it is more reason to begin saving.

He that has will receive more, he that does not have, even what he has will be taken away from him.

CHAPTER NINETEEN: WISDOM

Wisdom is so essential in attaining financial abundance. Beyond finances, wisdom is still key.

Proverbs 4:7 Wisdom *is* the principal thing; *therefore* get wisdom: and with all thy getting get understanding.

Wisdom is the important thing. And we are admonished to get wisdom. Then we are admonished to understand what we are getting.

Wisdom plays a critical role in financial abundance. How so? It helps individuals identify, create and take advantage of opportunities they never knew existed.

I discovered a scripture the other day that shocked me to the core. It showed that wisdom can build a house all by itself.

And before you say you do not have wisdom, watch carefully the scripture below:

1Co 1:30 But of him are ye in Christ Jesus, who of God is made unto us wisdom, and righteousness, and sanctification, and redemption:

Jesus has been made unto you wisdom. If you have him you have wisdom. Your problem may be that you did not know you had the very wisdom of God.

Since you did not know, that wisdom has remained dormant in your life. However from today, you shall do financial exploits with the wisdom of God in your life.

Shout it to yourself. I have wisdom. I have the principal thing.

The wisdom of God is at work in your life. Financial abundance is yours in Jesus name. You have clarity of thought and clarity of vision. You know exactly what to do. In Jesus name.

Let us get to the scripture I discovered.

Proverbs 24:3 Through wisdom is an house builded; and by understanding it is established:

A house is built through wisdom. It is established through understanding.

Think about it carefully. Even as you are reading, you have wisdom. The highest kind of wisdom. Divine wisdom. It is superior to earthly wisdom.

By that wisdom that you have, houses can be built.

My brother and my sister, if you ever convinced yourself that you didn't have what it takes to build a house, think again. Break that barrier.

WISDOM INVESTS IN ASSETS

An asset is whatever puts money into your pocket or bank account.

It is thus wisdom to have more assets as it will put more money into your pocket.

Whatever money you get, think of buying something that will put money into your pocket.

There are many things people hire or rent on a daily basis. Buy one or more of such things and let people rent from you and pay daily for it.

WISDOM AVOIDS INVESTMENT IN LIABILITIES

A liability is anything that takes money out of your pocket.

A lot of people are specialists in investing in liabilities.

They have so many liabilities that their liabilities alone can make them poor.

WISDOM SAVES FOR THE FUTURE

It is wisdom to save no matter how small your income is.

It shows you value your future. It shows you believe in a better tomorrow.

No matter how small your income is, you need to save till it gets to a point you can invest in an opportunity and make more money from it.

WISDOM CREATES MULTIPLE STREAMS OF INCOME

It is wisdom to have more than one source of income.

Therefore, make it a goal to create at least one different source of income every year. Presently I have about five sources of income.

There is no way financial abundance won't be my reality. Wisdom is working in my life.

This wisdom is creating financial abundance in my life on a daily basis.

Make use of wisdom in your life.

CHAPTER TWENTY: PRAYER AND ABUNDANCE

The issue of prayer cannot be underestimated in the area of finances.

Prayer does a lot of things after you have put the foundations in place.

Prayer is not what brings financial abundance. However it plays its part in ensuring that your income sources are discovered and are not hindered.

PRAYER OPENS YOUR MIND AND EYES TO OPPORTUNITY

Some of my income streams I discovered in a dream. I had prayed for my eyes to be opened to opportunities around me and sure enough, one day as I was asleep, I saw what could be a great income stream in a dream.

Prayer causes your mind to be sharp to receive ideas that can prosper you and make you financially abundant.

That is why prayer is key in the life of every believer believing for prosperity.

Prayer is a spiritual exercise and exposes you to a realm beyond the natural realm.

You are exposed to great ideas and empowerment that can take you to levels of abundance you never imagined.

If you are not a praying person, learn to pray. I have several books on prayer. I have two special ones on financial miracles. Do well to get them.

PRAYER CLEARS HINDRANCES

If you have not had a setback before, you have not begun in life. Most people have experienced setbacks in various areas including finances.

The successful and financially abundant always overcome such setbacks and difficult times.

When you pray, it deals with setbacks that will affect your income streams or opportunity even before they happen.

With such protection in prayer, you have less or no setbacks and things go well for you financially.

When you pray, things that set the finances of others back significantly like sicknesses, disasters, accidents hardly come your way.

By prayer, you deal with every spiritual enemy to your abundance.

PRAYER ALLOWS MEN TO GIVE TO YOU

As long as you are giving, men must give back to you.

If men are not giving back to you, understand that there is a hindrance. Greed and other spirits are hindering what must come to you.

That is why you must deal with these things in prayer.

Luke 6:38 Give, and it shall be given unto you; good measure, pressed down, and shaken together, and running over, shall men give into your bosom. For with the same measure that ye mete withal it shall be measured to you again.

Are you receiving more than you are giving? If not, there is something wrong somewhere.

You can deal with that which is wrong in prayer.

After praying, you exercise your faith and claim the amount you need.

PRAYER BRINGS PEOPLE AND OPPORTUNITY YOUR WAY

As you pray, you attract people and opportunities your way.

Some of the people who will bring you great financial opportunity, you will not even know them.

Some of the opportunities you will bump into, you will never know they existed.

That is the power of prayer. It brings you more than you imagined in prayer.

Your God is a good God. What you pray about, He does beyond imagination.

Just receive the answer and see great things happen in your finances.

Financial abundance is your portion. Be strong in faith and prayer.

JOIN MY FINANCIAL ABUNDANCE COACHING.

You have read this book and believe within yourself that you can achieve financial abundance. Everything within you tells you that you will make it.

All you need now is guidance to reach that destination.

You have read of the various people I have guided to achieve financial abundance in no time.

As you read, you believe my guidance can help you too.

You are right, I am willing to help you reach your financial goals.

This year I am taking on only ten people to help on a personal basis reach their financial goals.

- I will answer all your questions
- I will help you discover opportunities around you and take advantage of them

- I will draw a normal plan with you with strategies to achieve all your financial goals.
- I will then help you set your expanded financial goals and draw a workable plan to achieve it.
- I will encourage and pray for you all year through till you achieve your financial goal.
- What I did for others to achieve financial abundance, I will do same for you.

IS THE COACHING PROGRAM RIGHT FOR ME?

This program is perfect for you if you have ever said anything like;

- I want more out of life but I don't know how to go about it or what to do.

- I have goals but they are too big I don't know if I can ever reach it.

- I don't even know what I want, am confused.

- I have great ideas, but I don't know how to bring them to light.

- I know I can be financially abundant if only I know what to do.

- I give up easily and I need someone to guide me and encourage me and let me know I am on the right path.

This is an interactive coaching program that is designed to help you answer these questions and more and to help you achieve all your financial goals and dreams to enable you reach the level of financial abundance, fulfillment in life and secure a great future for your family, loved ones and the less privileged.

As soon as you join this program, you will be taught, trained and supported until your financial future is secured.

I will be there with you every step of the way, as you build, create and secure your dream life.

WHY SHOULD I JOIN?

Each time I talk to people about joining my coaching program, the first question they ask is "WHY"? In other not to leave you in the dark as to

why you should enroll in this program I have decided to put down few answers to that question.

* All the people who enrolled in this program last year experienced a major turnaround in their financial life. I have built my skills of motivation, encouragement, teaching and pushing the people who enroll till they achieve their goals.

* I will not coach you simply by asking you to read books or watch YouTube videos and so on. I will join you; hold your hands as we walk together through the dark until you get to light, where you will experience financial abundance, true wealth and fulfillment. We will use all communication sources to make sure the experience is as personal as possible.

DOES THE COACH HAVE THE NECESSARY EXPERIENCE TO HELP ME?

This is another common question I get when I invite people for the program. To be honest at first it wasn't easy convincing people to enroll because I had no one to point at that I have helped and taught and helped to achieve financial abundance except myself but that is not the case now because I have people flying high at the top I can point at... I will be glad to also you get to that level of abundance so you can start flying with the aircraft of financial abundance and sailing with the ship of financial freedom.

TESTIMONIES

The testimonies you are about to read are mind blowing, but they will be nothing compared to what you will receive as soon as you enroll because I have become wiser and gained more experience.
1. Before I attended this great program, both my life and my finances were in shambles. I was a passenger on earth. But after the first day of the program I began to notice a positive change and a

shift in my life. When Dr. Francis spoke, he interrupted the thoughts of failure and lack going on in my mind. He helped restore the belief in me that I could climb the ladder of success and get to the top. He helped change the program that was running in me and helped me become a conscious Creator of my future... After one month, I turned $100 into $3,000. You can read my book on Amazon titled; "SECRET TO HAVING ALL YOU WANT" I wrote that book after he helped me find my purpose in life and helped me establish my enterprise in less than 3 months. Today am happy to recommend this program to you, it will transform your life and finances.

   - MICHAEL ENDWELL

2. After I attended the financial coaching program last year 2016, in less than 3 months I started my own business and 3 months later I bought my own house... I recommend this program to anyone who wants more out of life.

- JAMES BARNABAS

3. Because of this financial coaching program, I was able to start my own business. Today I am very proud of where I am financially. My life would have still been a mess if not for this program. I will recommend this program to anyone especially women who want to attain financial freedom. I am a very young woman and what I have attained financially still remains a wonder to me. There are people you meet that just have a way of making your life so much better. Dr. Francis is one of them.
- POSH

4. What still keeps me wondering is how fast this program transformed me and my finances.
This program has turned my whole life around. Because of this Program I have moved from a struggling small business owner to one who employs people. I highly recommend this program...

\- STANLEY

After these testimonies and many more I decided to take action to help others who I feel need this transformation.

Seeing how fast this program transformed the lives of these individuals who when I met them were struggling financially, I decided that it's time for me to help you too to reach your financial goals and attain financial abundance...

HOW DO I ENROLL?

NOTE: I am only taking ten people. This is so because I want to make the program as effective as possible. I want to ensure I have enough time to work with the ten who really want financial abundance in no time.

If you want to be part of this number that will achieve financial abundance this year, send me a mail. My email is drfrancisjonah@gmail.com. Title your mail FINANCIAL ABUNDANCE COACHING.

Don't miss out.

DO I HAVE TO PAY?

There will be a small commitment fee so I can dedicate time to help you and also know your level OF seriousness about achieving your financial goals. Most people are only talk and take valuable contributions to their success for granted. It is the reason I want the best prepared people as much as possible.

For a whole year of personal coaching, you will need to commit $500.

This amount will be a token after few months of coaching because; you will make more than ten times of that amount. Some also will make a hundred and thousand times that amount as is evident from the testimonies.

TAKE ACTION NOW!

Send me an email to join this elite group that will create financial abundance in no time.

My email is **drfrancisjonah@gmail.com**. Title your mail FINANCIAL ABUNDANCE COACHING.

You know you have to make that decision now. Do not procrastinate. Send the email now.

My email is **drfrancisjonah@gmail.com**. Title your mail FINANCIAL ABUNDANCE COACHING. Abundance awaits you.

CHAPTER TWENTY ONE: IS PROSPERITY A BLESSING OR A CURSE?

I have heard many people lambast those who say and teach that you must prosper and be in health. They have spoken against those who say you must be financially abundant.

It has become so predominant that the question pops up. Is prosperity a blessing or a curse?

3John 1:2 Beloved, I wish above all things that thou mayest prosper and be in health, even as thy soul prospereth.

As we see in the scriptures, a man's prosperity is based on the prosperity of his soul. The soul consisting of his mind, will and emotions.

If these prosper and are in tune, prosperity will come easily to any man.

However if the realm of the soul or mind does not prosper, there will be difficulties in physical prosperity.

The wish of the writer above all else is that we prosper and be in health.

WHEN DID WEALTH BECOME A BAD THING?

To me, wealth in itself cannot be a bad thing. Perhaps how people use it is where the problem is.

If I use my wealth to make my life and those who come into contact with me better, I do not see anything wrong with.

If I use my wealth to give scholarships and provide medicine to those who cannot afford, I do not see the evil in my wealth.

POVERTY HAS DESTROYED MANY LIVES

I have seen first-hand how poverty has destroyed a lot of lives.

Students who could not go to school because of poverty.

Men and women and children without accommodation or health care because of poverty.

People dying young because of the stress of thinking of what they and their families will eat.

Nobody can convince me that poverty is a blessing.

How can anyone call not affording three square meals a day a blessing?

How can anyone convince me that my passion to be financially abundant to help solve the myriad of problems that confront my generation is wrong?

My mandate is to lend to nations. That is your mandate too.

This is not the time to call the good bad and the bad good.

Poverty can never be a blessing and prosperity can never be a curse.

YOU HAVE A CALLING

God has called you to be the light of the world.

You are a chosen generation with a divine assignment.

Matthew 5:14 Ye are the light of the world. A city that is set on an hill cannot be hid.

You are blessed with all the blessings in heaven.

You cannot afford to call a blessing a curse.

It is time to forge ahead and make impact in your generation.

You will control wealth.

It is your portion. Do not stoop for anything below that.

Regardless of your present circumstance, look at your calling and pursue it.

You were not called to be poor. You were called to be rich.

You were not called to lack, you were called to abundance.

You were not called to beg, you were called to lend.

You were not called to manage, you were called to multiply.

Prosperity is a blessing, embrace it.

IF YOU HAVE SEEN POVERTY BEFORE, YOU WILL STRIVE TO WALK YOUR CALLING

Anyone who has seen true poverty before will strive to be abundant. Not for themselves but to help the helpless.

When you see children who have not eaten for weeks, not because they are not hungry, but because they cannot afford a meal.

When you see adults who have to abandon their families because they can no longer provide for them.

When you see such things you will understand why today the calling upon your life is greater.

Arise for your calling beckons. Break through into the realm of financial abundance.

A child is waiting for you, a family is waiting for you. You have a calling.

CHAPTER TWENTY TWO: CAPTAIN AND FARMER

One Bible story that fascinates me is the story of Potiphar.

Potiphar was an officer of Pharaoh. He had Joseph in his house as a servant. Joseph was in charge of all his business.

Everything he had prospered because the Lord was with Joseph. The blessing of God was upon Joseph. And that blessing reflected in the house of Potiphar.

Genesis 39:3 And his master saw that the LORD *was* with him, and that the LORD made all that he did to prosper in his hand.

Genesis 39:4 And Joseph found grace in his sight, and he served him: and he made him overseer over his house, and all *that* he had he put into his hand.

Genesis 39:5 And it came to pass from the time *that* he had made him overseer in his house, and over all that he had, that the LORD blessed the

Egyptian's house for Joseph's sake; and the blessing of the LORD was upon all that he had in the house, and in the field.

A CAPTAIN HAD A FARM

Even though Potiphar was a captain and earned money for that position, he was also a farmer.

…………… and the blessing of the LORD was upon all that he had in the house, and in the field.Genesis 39:5

This scripture states clearly that Potiphar had a field. Having a field is synonymous with having a farm.

It is worth noting that even a rich captain believed in extra income.

He believed in creating employment for others.

He believed he could achieve more if he helped others also achieve what they wanted.

Potiphar's farm supplied extra income or provision for his household.

This is an unbeliever understanding the laws of prosperity.

An unbeliever taking advantage of seed time and harvest.

His farm brought multiplication of his seed.

The best part is that because Joseph was there he prospered even more.

I won't be surprised If he had other ventures in the house.

He had clearly been trained in how to create abundance.

YOU CAN HAVE MORE THAN 24 HOURS A DAY

As individuals, we all have 24 hours in a day.

Some however are enjoying more than 24 hours a day.

How are they doing it you say?

When a man takes advantage of an opportunity and the opportunity is so big that he needs to employ people to work for him or with him to take full advantage of the opportunity, he begins to exchange money for their time.

If ten people work 8 hours a day for you, that is 80 hours a day for you.

If you were working alone, you can never put in 80 hours a day.

Men who identify and take advantage of opportunity always have more than 24 hours in a day. It is simple they are using other peoples time.

NOTHING IS TOO BIG

When you walk with small minded people for a long time, small things look big.

When you walk with non-achievers for a long time, you think your dream is too big.

Never think your dream of financial abundance is too big. It is more than possible.

MY STORY

For a long time I was holding a program. I had people helping me for the program. Some brought in one person, others brought in 2 people maximum. One day a young man came in that brought 17 people for the program. His name is Michael Endwell, do well to read his books. He has fire in his bosom.

If you have ten of the people who bring a maximum 2 people, you will think your dream is impossible.

When you begin to have those who bring 17 people, you will realize that the old people nearly limited you and made you think your dream was impossible.

All dreams are possible. Surround yourself and pray for the right people to help you achieve your dream.

MY BROTHER'S STORY

My brother is a great businessman. He told me the other time that he met a client and when the client asked for his fees, he said $1,500.

The client thought for a while and said $1,500 was quite an amount to charge per month, however it was worth it. He then asked my brother how many months in advance he must pay.

My brother in turn told him that the $1,500 was for a year not a month like the client thought.

That day my brother learned a great lesson. When you walk with small and stingy clients for a long time, they affect your view of what charges are possible in business.

Dream big. Pray to attract the right people. You will go places. In Jesus name.

CHAPTER TWENTY THREE: POSSESS YOUR POSSESSIONS

Possess your possessions simply means take what is yours.

Let us see a scripture that explains the statement:

Joshua 18:1 And the whole congregation of the children of Israel assembled together at Shiloh, and set up the tabernacle of the congregation there. And the land was subdued before them.

Joshua 18:2 And there remained among the children of Israel seven tribes, which had not yet received their inheritance.

Joshua 18:3 And Joshua said unto the children of Israel, How long *are* ye slack to go to possess the land, which the LORD God of your fathers hath given you?

In the scripture, we realize that out of the twelve tribes of Israel, five had taken what God had given to them.

Seven of the tribes were still waiting to possess their possession.

What they were waiting for, only they can tell.

FINANCIAL ABUNDANCE IS ALREADY AVAILABLE

In your country, in your community there are several millions of dollars in people's pockets and bank accounts.

Every day, they spend millions of this amount. The amounts they spend go to someone's pocket.

The question you should be asking yourself is that "why is part of that money not coming to me?"

You see, the abundance you need is out there, why is it that you are not partaking in it.

Why are you not possessing your possession?

I remember how after teaching three young men the amount of money in their community, they found an opportunity to partake in the abundance.

MY SONS SUCCEEEDED

Within one week of speaking to them, they found an opportunity and became partakers of the abundance in their community.

When I asked them what had changed, all they could say was that our eyes have been opened.

Today they are making so much more than their salaries part time.

They possessed their possessions. What are you waiting for? Go for your portion of abundance.

Wherever people are spending money, you can have your portion of the money.

AMBITION IS A BETTER FOUNDATION THAN MONEY

Ambition should be your starting point. You must desire to be financially abundant and that desire must be great enough to move you to take massive action.

A man with ambition and without money can make so much money.

Ambition and desire cannot be bought. It is something you must have within you.

Pursuit is the proof of your desire.

If you really want to be financially abundant, then pursue it.

LET THE BLESSING WORK

Put the blessing of God to work in your life. Do not let your job or business determine your financial abundance. Determine it first and let the blessing take you to that financial level by taking advantage of several opportunities.

MENTORS AND COACHES

A mentor has already achieved whatever you want to achieve.

He or she will guide you to achieve that which he or she has achieved.

A mentor will save you years of trial and error.

In my personal experience, many of my sons and daughters achieved financial abundance within three months to one year of my guidance.

That is the impact of a mentor on the life of any individual.

JOIN MYFINANCIAL ABUNDANCE COACHING.

You have read this book and believe within yourself that you can achieve financial abundance.

Everything within you tells you that you will make it.

All you need now is guidance to reach that destination.

You have read of the various people I have guided to achieve financial abundance in no time.

As you read, you believe my guidance can help you too.

You are right, I am willing to help you reach your financial goals.

This year I am taking on only ten people to help on a personal basis reach their financial goals.

- I will answer all your questions
- I will help you discover opportunities around you and take advantage of them
- I will draw a normal plan with you with strategies to achieve all your financial goals.

- I will then help you set your expanded financial goals and draw a workable plan to achieve it.
- I will encourage and pray for you all year through till you achieve your financial goal.
- What I did for others to achieve financial abundance, I will do same for you.

IS THE COACHING PROGRAM RIGHT FOR ME?

This program is perfect for you if you have ever said anything like;

- I want more out of life but I don't know how to go about it or what to do.
- I have goals but they are too big I don't know if I can ever reach it.
- I don't even know what I want, am confused.
- I have great ideas, but I don't know how to bring them to light.
- I know I can be financially abundant if only I know what to do.

- I give up easily and I need someone to guide me and encourage me and let me know I am on the right path.

This is an interactive coaching program that is designed to help you answer these questions and more and to help you achieve all your financial goals and dreams to enable you reach the level of financial abundance, fulfillment in life and secure a great future for your family, loved ones and the less privileged.

As soon as you join this program, you will be taught, trained and supported until your financial future is secured.

I will be there with you every step of the way, as you build, create and secure your dream life.

WHY SHOULD I JOIN?

Each time I talk to people about joining my coaching program, the first question they ask is "WHY"? In other not to leave you in the dark as to

why you should enroll in this program I have decided to put down few answers to that question.

* All the people who enrolled in this program last year experienced a major turnaround in their financial life. I have built my skills of motivation, encouragement, teaching and pushing the people who enroll till they achieve their goals.

* I will not coach you simply by asking you to read books or watch YouTube videos and so on. I will join you; hold your hands as we walk together through the dark until you get to light, where you will experience financial abundance, true wealth and fulfillment. We will use all communication sources to make sure the experience is as personal as possible.

DOES THE COACH HAVE THE NECESSARY EXPERIENCE TO HELP ME?

This is another common question I get when I invite people for the program. To be honest at first it wasn't easy convincing people to enroll because I had no one to point at that I have helped and taught and helped to achieve financial abundance except myself but that is not the case now because I have people flying high at the top I can point at... I will be glad to also you get to that level of abundance so you can start flying with the aircraft of financial abundance and sailing with the ship of financial freedom.

TESTIMONIES

The testimonies you are about to read are mind blowing, but they will be nothing compared to what you will receive as soon as you enroll because I have become wiser and gained more experience.
1. Before I attended this great program, both my life and my finances were in shambles. I was a passenger on earth. But after the first day of the program I began to notice a positive change and a

shift in my life. When Dr. Francis spoke, he interrupted the thoughts of failure and lack going on in my mind. He helped restore the belief in me that I could climb the ladder of success and get to the top. He helped change the program that was running in me and helped me become a conscious Creator of my future... After one month, I turned $100 into $3,000. You can read my book on Amazon titled; "SECRET TO HAVING ALL YOU WANT" I wrote that book after he helped me find my purpose in life and helped me establish my enterprise in less than 3 months. Today am happy to recommend this program to you, it will transform your life and finances.

   - MICHAEL ENDWELL

2. After I attended the financial coaching program last year 2016, in less than 3 months I started my own business and 3 months later I bought my own house... I recommend this program to anyone who wants more out of life.

- JAMES BARNABAS

3. Because of this financial coaching program, I was able to start my own business. Today I am very proud of where I am financially. My life would have still been a mess if not for this program. I will recommend this program to anyone especially women who want to attain financial freedom. I am a very young woman and what I have attained financially still remains a wonder to me. There are people you meet that just have a way of making your life so much better. Dr. Francis is one of them.
 - POSH

4. What still keeps me wondering is how fast this program transformed me and my finances.
This program has turned my whole life around. Because of this Program I have moved from a struggling small business owner to one who employs people. I highly recommend this program...

\- STANLEY

After these testimonies and many more I decided to take action to help others who I feel need this transformation.
Seeing how fast this program transformed the lives of these individuals who when I met them were struggling financially, I decided that it's time for me to help you too to reach your financial goals and attain financial abundance...

HOW DO I ENROLL?
NOTE: I am only taking ten people. This is so because I want to make the program as effective as possible. I want to ensure I have enough time to work with the ten who really want financial abundance in no time.
If you want to be part of this number that will achieve financial abundance this year, send me a mail. My email is drfrancisjonah@gmail.com. Title your mail FINANCIAL ABUNDANCE COACHING.

Don't miss out.

There will be a small commitment fee so I can dedicate time to help you and also know your level OF seriousness about achieving your financial goals. Most people are only talk and take valuable contributions to their success for granted. It is the reason I want the best prepared people as much as possible.

For a whole year of personal coaching, you will need to commit $500.

This amount will be a token after few months of coaching because; you will make more than ten times of that amount. Some also will make a hundred and thousand times that amount as is evident from the testimonies.

TAKE ACTION NOW!

Send me an email to join this elite group that will create financial abundance in no time.

My email is **drfrancisjonah@gmail.com.** Title your mail FINANCIAL ABUNDANCE COACHING.

You know you have to make that decision now. Do not procrastinate. Send the email now.

My email is **drfrancisjonah@gmail.com**. Title your mail FINANCIAL ABUNDANCE COACHING. Abundance awaits you.

CHAPTER TWENTY FOUR: A COSTTLY MISTAKE MANY MAKE

I have realized a costly mistake most people make.

I made this mistake some time ago in my life and it really hindered me.

The mistake is that they let their bosses or business determine their level of financial abundance.

For the past six years, the money they earn is the money their bosses have determined they are worth.

I keep advising people to determine how much they want in a month or a year before even getting a job.

When you determine you financial target, let us say $10,000 a month and your job pays $2,000.

Do not panic, understand that there is more work to be done.

This is the time to put the blessing of God to work in your life.

Many people will just limit themselves to the $2,000 and manage it.

Not you. You will keep looking for opportunities to make the difference of $8,000 till you make it.

You may not achieve the extra $8,000 in a month or a year. Maybe you will get there in two years.

The good news is that you will definitely get there. If you were waiting for your boss, you will never get them.

However as you have taken responsibility, you will get there.

When you get there, you will realize that you are making four times your full time income elsewhere part time.

That is when you can decide to continue working full time or enjoy the comforts financial abundance brings a man.

Do not make the mistake of limiting yourself to what people think you are worth.

Determine your worth and work to get there. You are blessed.

CHAPTER TWENTY FIVE: MY PRAYER FOR YOU

PRAYER

Father I thank you that you always hear me. I thank you for your love and your kindness.

I decree that whoever has read this book that is sick in any part of their body receives healing right now.

I command pain to leave. I command wholeness in bodies right now.

I decree that organs that are defective or unavailable be replaced right now in Jesus name.

I decree that tests that are contrary to the word of God are overturned in Jesus name.

I speak the power and anointing of God into bodies right now.

The spirit of God is vitalizing bodies right now.

Jobs are released, finances are released, and guidance is released.

I decree that whatever miracle you need right now is released to you in Jesus name.

Angels are released for your special case. I see them bring your own answers right now.

Satan take your hands of God's property. I rebuke you and every hindrance in the way of the answers that are available to these ones in Jesus name. Take your hands off their children, off their finances, of their marriages, off their promotion and increase, off their progress in Jesus name.

Experience extreme grace and favor in your going out and in your coming in.

Your way is prosperous. Good news surrounds your every step in Jesus name.

Dominion is yours in Jesus name. Master your circumstances and situations that come your way in Jesus mighty name.

Thank you Father, thank you Lord. I sense the strong impartation of the power and favor of God. Great grace and abundance is released right now.

Now start giving God your highest praise, it is done.

PLEASE NOTE

Please leave a good review of the book as well as testimonies so that others can be blessed by this book. I will also like to hear from you and pray for you.

There are other books by me Francis Jonah that you must read.

Just search for my name on amazon.com and scroll through my books for more revelation that will help you do the impossible.

My email is drfrancisjonah@gmail.com

FREE BOOK

The free book "all things are possible is still available"

Send me a mail and receive your free copy.

JOIN MYFINANCIAL ABUNDANCE COACHING.

You have read this book and believe within yourself that you can achieve financial abundance. Everything within you tells you that you will make it.

All you need now is guidance to reach that destination.

You have read of the various people I have guided to achieve financial abundance in no time.

As you read, you believe my guidance can help you too.

You are right, I am willing to help you reach your financial goals.

This year I am taking on only ten people to help on a personal basis reach their financial goals.

- I will answer all your questions
- I will help you discover opportunities around you and take advantage of them
- I will draw a normal plan with you with strategies to achieve all your financial goals.
- I will then help you set your expanded financial goals and draw a workable plan to achieve it.
- I will encourage and pray for you all year through till you achieve your financial goal.
- What I did for others to achieve financial abundance, I will do same for you.

IS THE COACHING PROGRAM RIGHT FOR ME?

This program is perfect for you if you have ever said anything like;
- I want more out of life but I don't know how to go about it or what to do.
- I have goals but they are too big I don't know if I can ever reach it.
- I don't even know what I want, am confused.
- I have great ideas, but I don't know how to bring them to light.
- I know I can be financially abundant if only I know what to do.
- I give up easily and I need someone to guide me and encourage me and let me know I am on the right path.

This is an interactive coaching program that is designed to help you answer these questions and more and to help you achieve all your financial goals and dreams to enable you reach the level of financial abundance, fulfillment in life and secure a great future for your family, loved ones and the less privileged.

As soon as you join this program, you will be taught, trained and supported until your financial future is secured.

I will be there with you every step of the way, as you build, create and secure your dream life.

Each time I talk to people about joining my coaching program, the first question they ask is "WHY"? In other not to leave you in the dark as to why you should enroll in this program I have decided to put down few answers to that question.

* All the people who enrolled in this program last year experienced a major turnaround in their financial life. I have built my skills of motivation, encouragement, teaching and pushing the people who enroll till they achieve their goals.

* I will not coach you simply by asking you to read books or watch YouTube videos and so on. I will join you; hold your hands as we walk together through the dark until you get to light, where you will experience financial abundance, true wealth and fulfillment. We will use all communication sources to make sure the experience is as personal as possible.

DOES THE COACH HAVE THE NECESSARY EXPERIENCE TO HELP ME?

This is another common question I get when I invite people for the program. To be honest at first it wasn't easy convincing people to enroll because I had no one to point at that I have helped and taught and helped to achieve financial abundance except myself but that is not the case now because I have people flying high at the top I can point at... I will be glad to also you get to that level of abundance so you can start flying with the aircraft of financial abundance and sailing with the ship of financial freedom.

TESTIMONIES

The testimonies you are about to read are mind blowing, but they will be nothing compared to what you will receive as soon as you enroll because I have become wiser and gained more experience.
1. Before I attended this great program, both my life and my finances were in shambles. I was a passenger on earth. But after the first day of the program I began to notice a positive change and a shift in my life. When Dr. Francis spoke, he interrupted the thoughts of failure and lack going on in my mind. He helped restore the belief in me that I could climb the ladder of success and get to the top. He helped change the program that was running in me and helped me become a conscious Creator of my future... After one month, I turned $100 into $3,000. You can read my book on Amazon titled; "SECRET TO HAVING ALL YOU

WANT" I wrote that book after he helped me find my purpose in life and helped me establish my enterprise in less than 3 months. Today am happy to recommend this program to you, it will transform your life and finances.

    - MICHAEL ENDWELL

2. After I attended the financial coaching program last year 2016, in less than 3 months I started my own business and 3 months later I bought my own house... I recommend this program to anyone who wants more out of life.

    - JAMES BARNABAS

3. Because of this financial coaching program, I was able to start my own business. Today I am very proud of where I am financially. My life would have still been a mess if not for this program. I will recommend this program to anyone especially women who want to attain financial freedom. I am a very young woman and what I have attained

financially still remains a wonder to me. There are people you meet that just have a way of making your life so much better. Dr. Francis is one of them.
 - POSH

4. What still keeps me wondering is how fast this program transformed me and my finances.
This program has turned my whole life around. Because of this Program I have moved from a struggling small business owner to one who employs people. I highly recommend this program...
   - STANLEY

After these testimonies and many more I decided to take action to help others who I feel need this transformation.
Seeing how fast this program transformed the lives of these individuals who when I met them were struggling financially, I decided that it's time for me

to help you too to reach your financial goals and attain financial abundance...

HOW DO I ENROLL?

NOTE: I am only taking ten people. This is so because I want to make the program as effective as possible. I want to ensure I have enough time to work with the ten who really want financial abundance in no time.

If you want to be part of this number that will achieve financial abundance this year, send me a mail. My email is drfrancisjonah@gmail.com. Title your mail FINANCIAL ABUNDANCE COACHING. Don't miss out.

DO I HAVE TO PAY?

There will be a small commitment fee so I can dedicate time to help you and also know your level OF seriousness about achieving your financial goals. Most people are only talk and take valuable contributions to their success for granted. It is the reason I want the best prepared people as much as possible.

For a whole year of personal coaching, you will need to commit $500.

This amount will be a token after few months of coaching because; you will make more than ten times of that amount. Some also will make a hundred and thousand times that amount as is evident from the testimonies.

TAKE ACTION NOW!

Send me an email to join this elite group that will create financial abundance in no time.

My email is **drfrancisjonah@gmail.com.** Title your mail FINANCIAL ABUNDANCE COACHING.

You know you have to make that decision now. Do not procrastinate. Send the email now.

My email is **drfrancisjonah@gmail.com**. Title your mail FINANCIAL ABUNDANCE COACHING. Abundance awaits you.

Made in United States
North Haven, CT
30 October 2022

26102190R00146